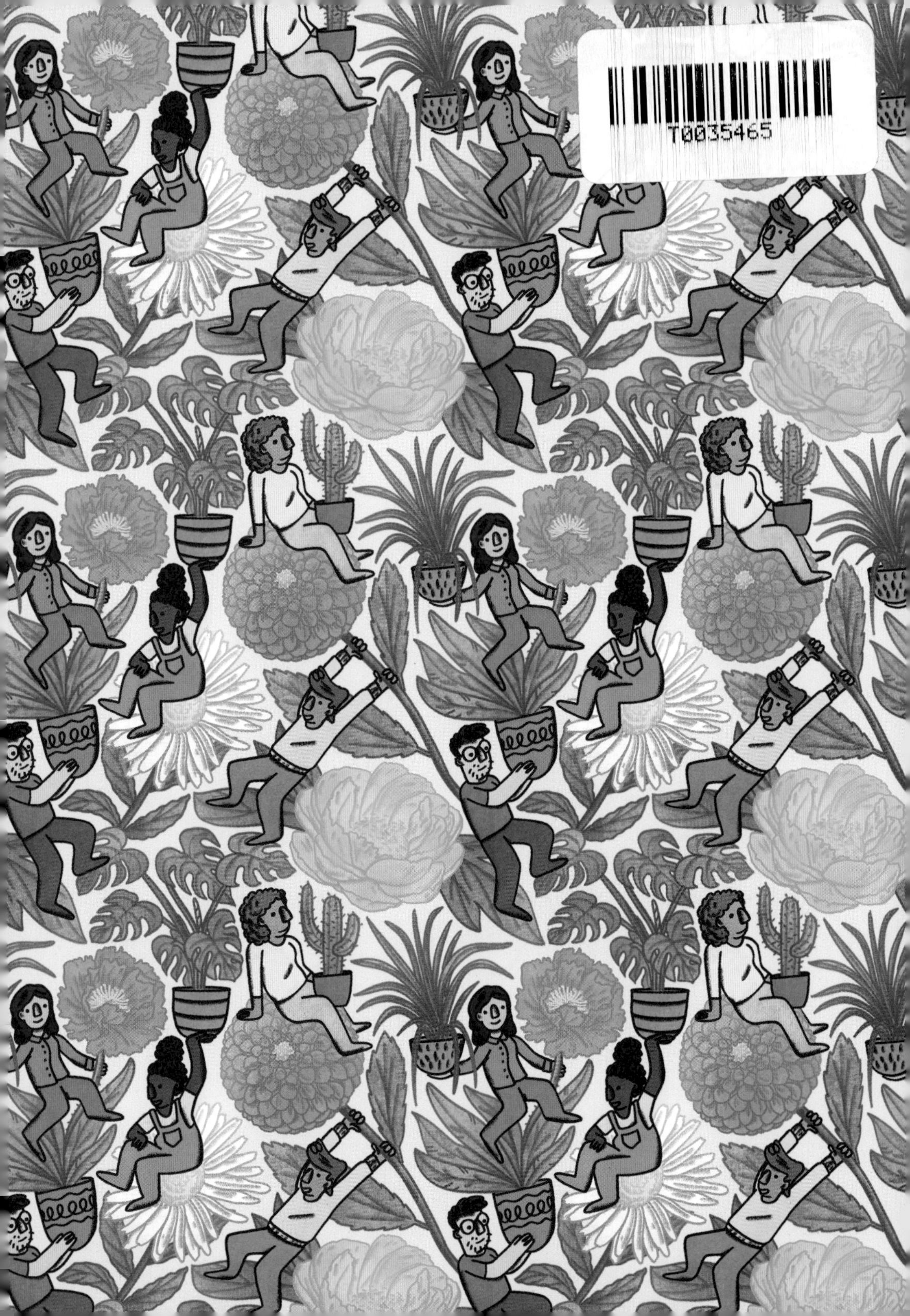

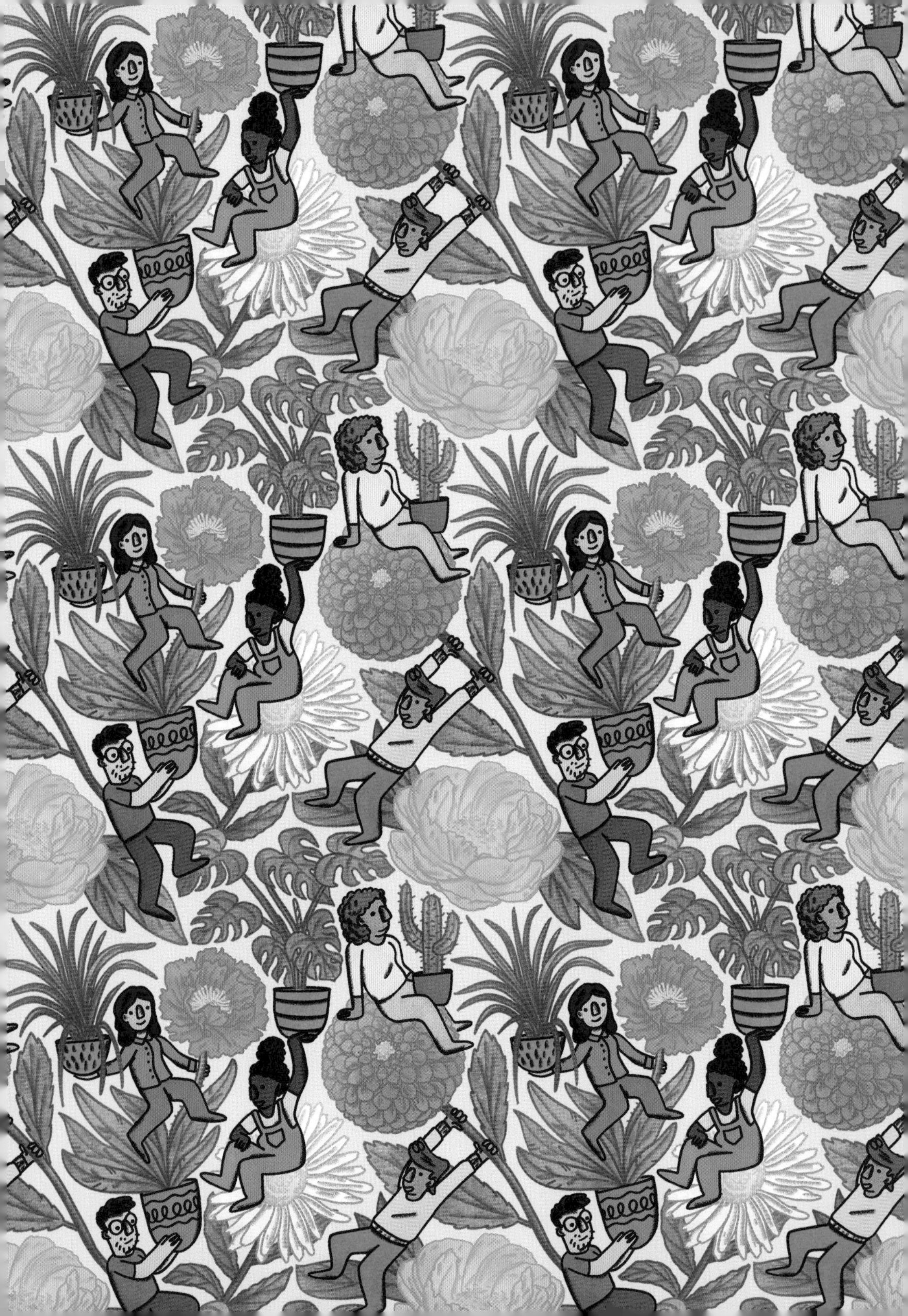

PLEASE GROW

GROW

LESSONS ON THRIVING FOR PLANTS (AND PEOPLE)

ALEX TESTERE

Clarkson Potter/Publishers
New York

THIS IS A BOOK ABOUT PLANTS.

It's about roots and leaves
and branches and buds—

BUT IT'S ALSO A BOOK ABOUT YOU.

It's about the tender, little seeds of things you've dreamed up—and the lush, magnificent trees they can become if you help them along. It's about learning when to grow with vigor and when to be still, when to dig deep and when to burst into bloom.

Even the largest living tree on Earth, a giant redwood in Sequoia National Park, began as a seed no larger than a pea that drifted down from the canopy more than two millennia ago.

YOU'VE GOT TO START SOMEWHERE.

SO WHY NOT HERE?

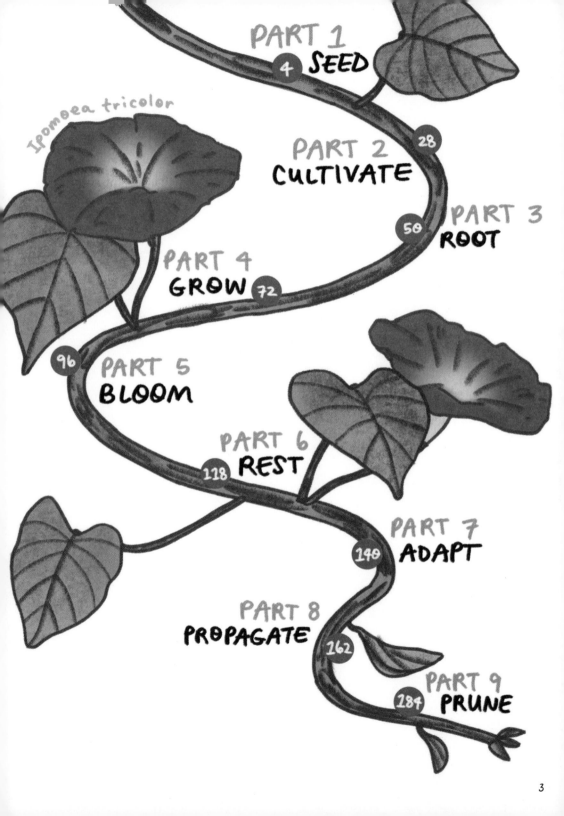

Ipomoea tricolor

PART 1

SEED

CONSIDER THE SEED.

SMALL,
HARD,
LIFELESS.

YOU MIGHT MISS IT
COMPLETELY IF YOU DON'T
KNOW WHERE TO LOOK.

Some seeds are impossibly small, like those of orchids, which disperse their weightless seeds into the air like dust.

Cocos nucifera

Phalaenopsis schilleriana

But even the most massive seeds, like coconuts, are still small enough to hold in your hand.

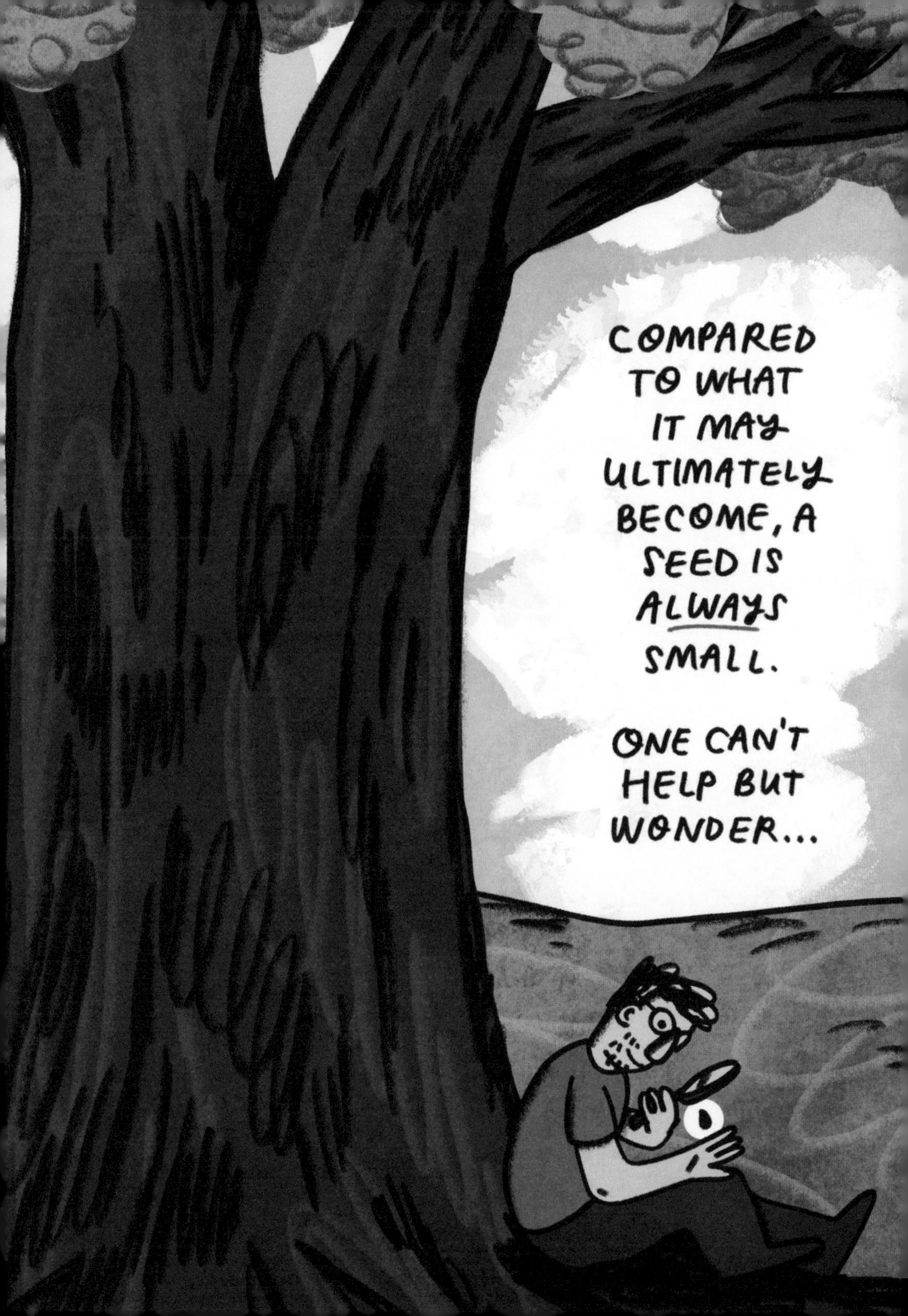
COMPARED TO WHAT IT MAY ULTIMATELY BECOME, A SEED IS ALWAYS SMALL.
ONE CAN'T HELP BUT WONDER...

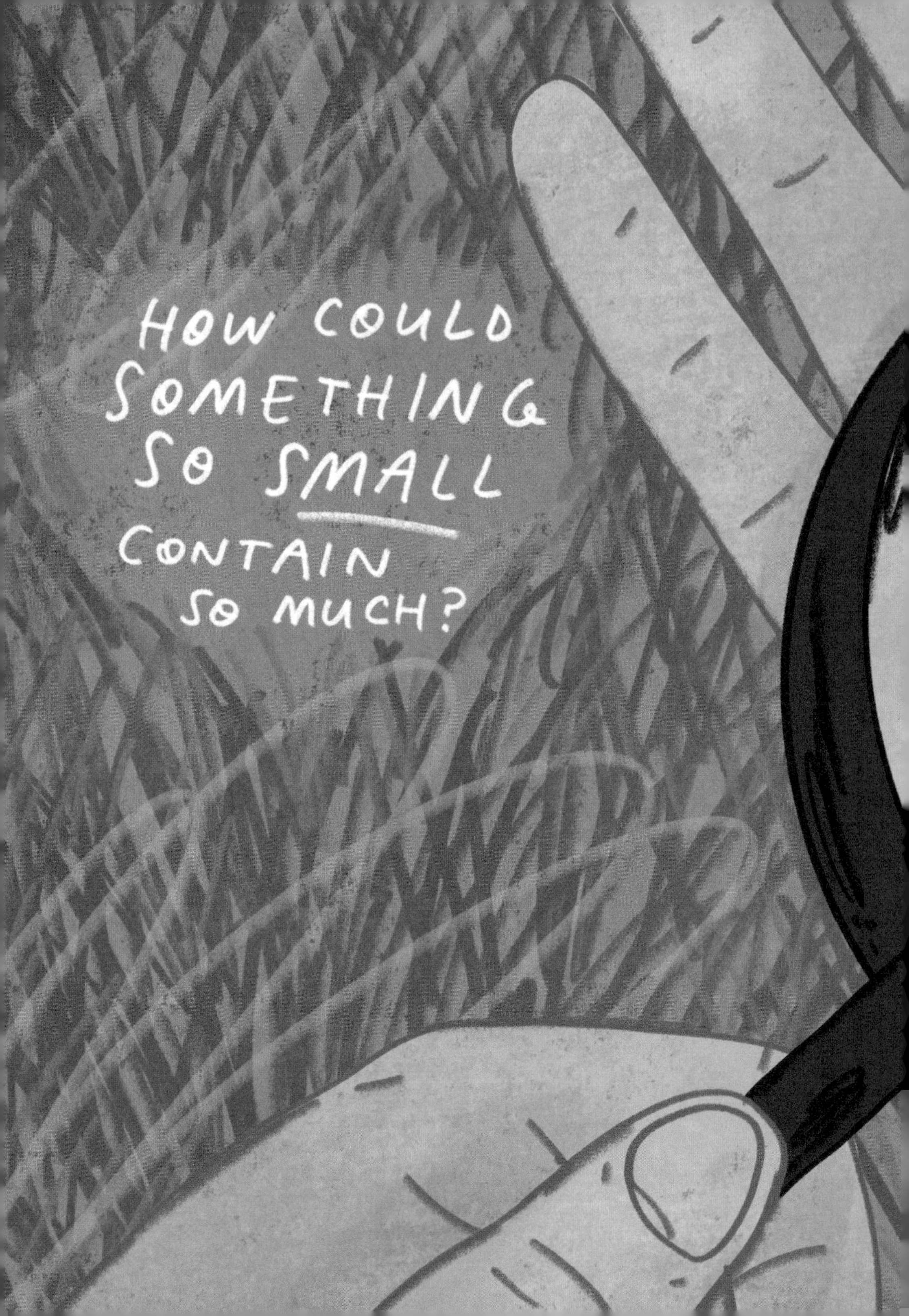
HOW COULD SOMETHING SO SMALL CONTAIN SO MUCH?

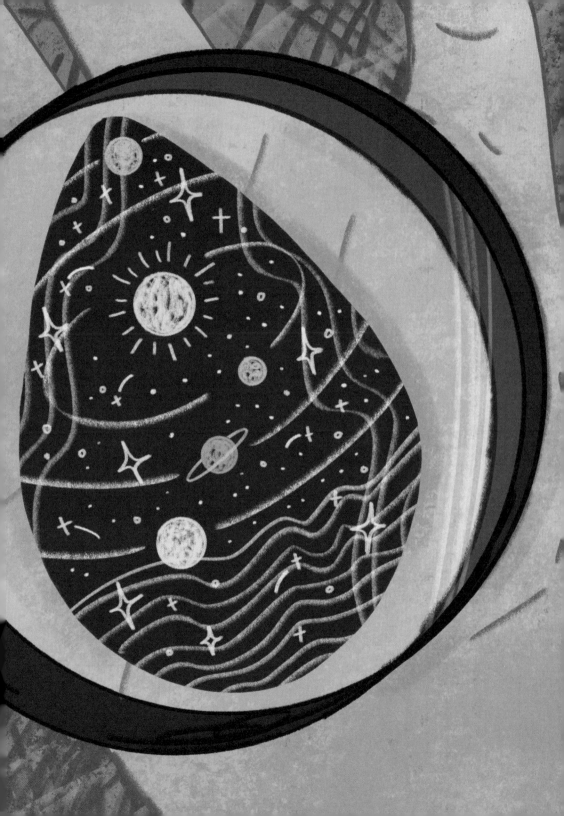

But that is precisely the magic of the seed. It is compact, inert, silent—just waiting for the right circumstances to arise.

Whether it's by wind or water or consumption by a hungry animal, a seed's very design invites it to be pushed along by whatever exterior forces interact with it.

A SEED WANTS TO SUCCEED. IT JUST NEEDS A LITTLE HELP.

ALL SORTS OF GREAT THINGS BEGIN AS SEEDS:

ideas

watermelons

rutabagas

sunflowers

babies

ancient architectural marvels

every work of art that ever existed

A seed can grow into almost anything you can imagine. Maybe yours is a house by the beach or a career as a paleobotanist. Maybe it's a bakery or an MBA or a handmade ceramic bowl. Maybe it's just a big, juicy tomato.

No matter how big or small a plant (or a dream) may be, it all starts with a seed.

HOW TO GROW SOMETHING FROM A SEED

STEP 1
FIND A SEED

First ask yourself:
What type of seed am I looking for?

Seeds that grow into vegetables or flowers are pretty easy to come by. But those other seeds—the ones that grow into families or careers or books or businesses—can be a bit harder to find. You might even have one already, tucked in the back of your mind, waiting for you to work up the courage to plant it.

IF YOU DON'T HAVE A SEED YET,
THERE ARE PLENTY OF PLACES
ONE MIGHT APPEAR.

BETWEEN THE PAGES
OF A JOURNAL

IN THE
SHOWER

ONE HOUR INTO A VERY
SERIOUS FILM ABOUT
SOMETHING ELSE ENTIRELY

OUT IN THE MIDDLE OF A LAKE, BUT ONLY AFTER 20 MINUTES OF GOOD STARING

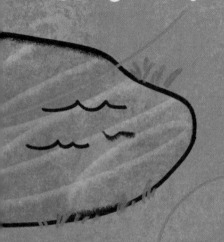

CROSSING THE STREET

UNDER YOUR SHOE

IN THE BAKING AISLE AT THE SUPERMARKET

Seeds—like ideas—don't always appear where (or when) we expect them to. They are abundant and they are everywhere, but they are elusive.

Have you ever thought, "I should try that," and then found some excuse not to?

THE BIG ONE!

THAT

IS A

SEED.

Have you ever wondered, "how does this work?" and then never found out?

THAT IS A SEED TOO.

Turn over every stone. Pay attention to the random thoughts that pop into your head. Investigate every little thing that interests you. A seed is waiting for you. You just have to claim it.

PLANT THE SEED

SEEDS NEED SOMEWHERE TO GROW.

They can be resilient, but even the strongest
seeds require three basic elements.

SOIL

WATER

SUNLIGHT

These are absolutely crucial for seeds that grow into
vegetables and flowers. It turns out, they're also
quite helpful for those more elusive seeds, too.

SOIL GIVES THE SEED
SOMETHING TO ROOT IN, A FIRM
FOOTING TO BEGIN ITS LIFE.

Take a walk in the woods. Feel your feet pressing
into solid ground and feel the earth pushing back.
Consider how it feels to be so supported.

WATER HELPS SIGNAL TO THE SEED THAT IT'S TIME TO GET STARTED.

Take your seed to the beach. Throw yourselves in the sea. A bath works, too. Hydrate. Submerge yourself. Consider how it feels to be held afloat.

SUNLIGHT PROVIDES THE WARMTH AND ENERGY REQUIRED TO FUEL THE SEED'S EARLIEST GROWTH.

Find a sunbeam anywhere you can. Enter it, face first. Feel the sun on your skin. Soak it all up. Consider how it feels to be so warm and glowing and alive.

STEP 3
PROTECT THE SEEDLING

A seedling is delicate. Any number of foes could cut its life short before it's even begun—whether they mean to or not. Be wary of potential predators and build a fence to keep them at bay.

hungry squirrels

curious birds

judgmental neighbors

OMG I HAVE AN IDEA*!

*YOUR IDEA

self-interested "friends"

your own inner saboteur

THESE WILL ONLY GET IN THE WAY.

Fraxinus
pennsylvanica

22

CHECK IN ON THE SEEDLING EVERY DAY.

IN ITS EARLY STAGES, EVEN THE STRONGEST SEEDLING CAN PERISH FROM NEGLECT.

Hoya carnosa

REST ASSURED, IF YOU DO LOSE A SEEDLING, YOU CAN ALWAYS START OVER.

BUT THEN, WELL, YOU HAVE TO START OVER.

AND YOU'VE COME SO FAR! BEST TO HOLD ON TO WHAT YOU'VE GOT.

ONCE THE SEEDLING IS SAFE, ASK FOR HELP.

While keeping out anything that might harm your seedling, invite in anyone who might offer helpful advice.

friendly beekeepers

Lifelong friends

a trusted mentor

someone you've never met before but they inspire you greatly and maybe they'd like to grab coffee sometime???

(It's worth a shot!)

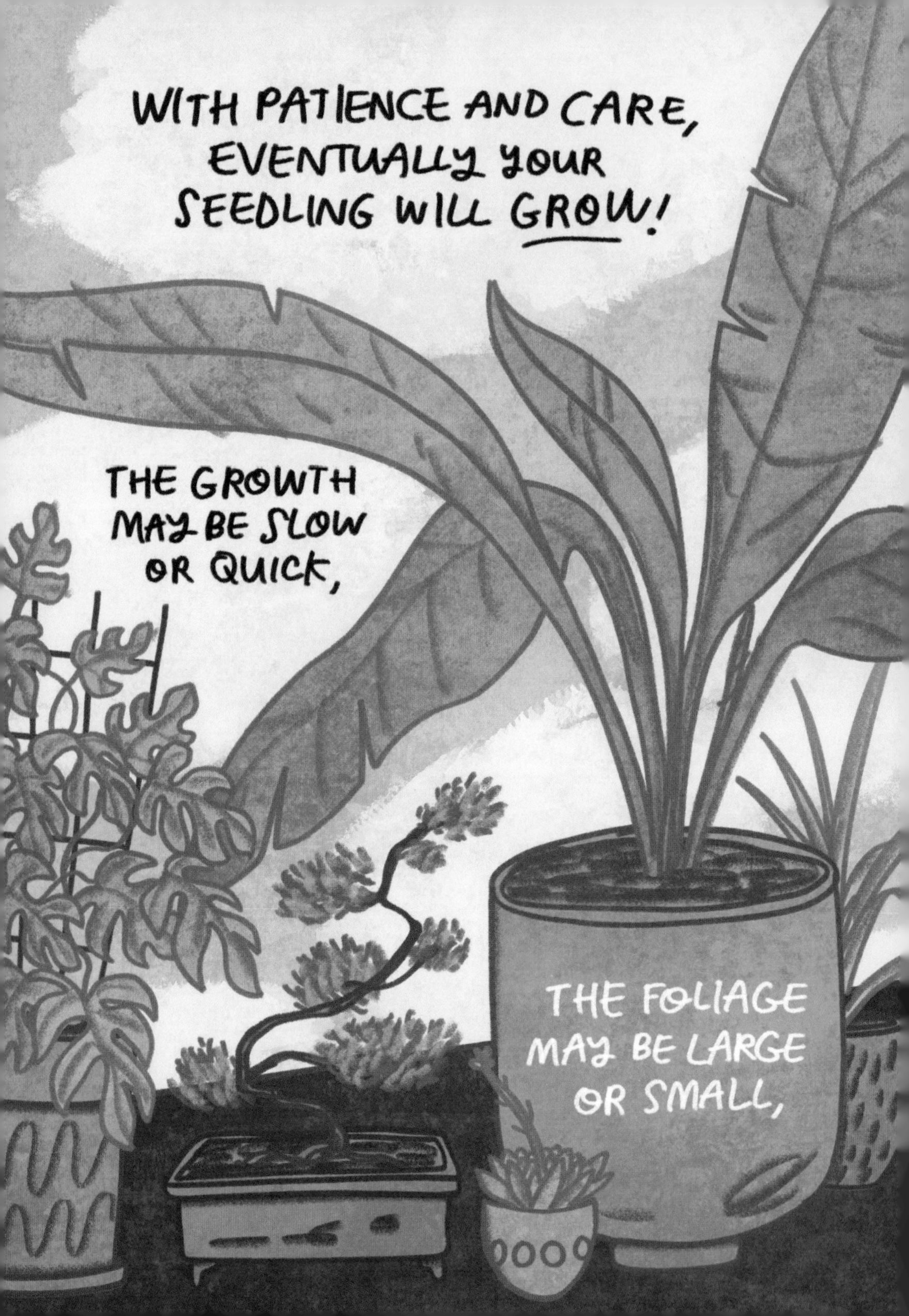
WITH PATIENCE AND CARE, EVENTUALLY YOUR SEEDLING WILL GROW!
THE GROWTH MAY BE SLOW OR QUICK,
THE FOLIAGE MAY BE LARGE OR SMALL,

BUT IT WILL BE GROWING.
AND IT WILL BE YOURS.

WHAT COMES NEXT IS
ENTIRELY UP TO YOU.

PART 2

CULTIVATE

PLANTING A SEED IS ONLY THE BEGINNING.

Where it's planted and how the earth is cultivated around it will largely determine the plant's final shape.

Something as subtle as a shift in
the soil's acidity can turn hydrangea
blossoms from pink to blue.

Hydrangea
macrophylla

IT ALL COMES DOWN TO SOIL.

Soil fixes nutrients in the ground so they're always available. It's a solid foundation, the place where we choose to put down roots. It's the well from which we draw inspiration, motivation, and fulfillment.

AND IT'S A LOT MORE THAN JUST DIRT.

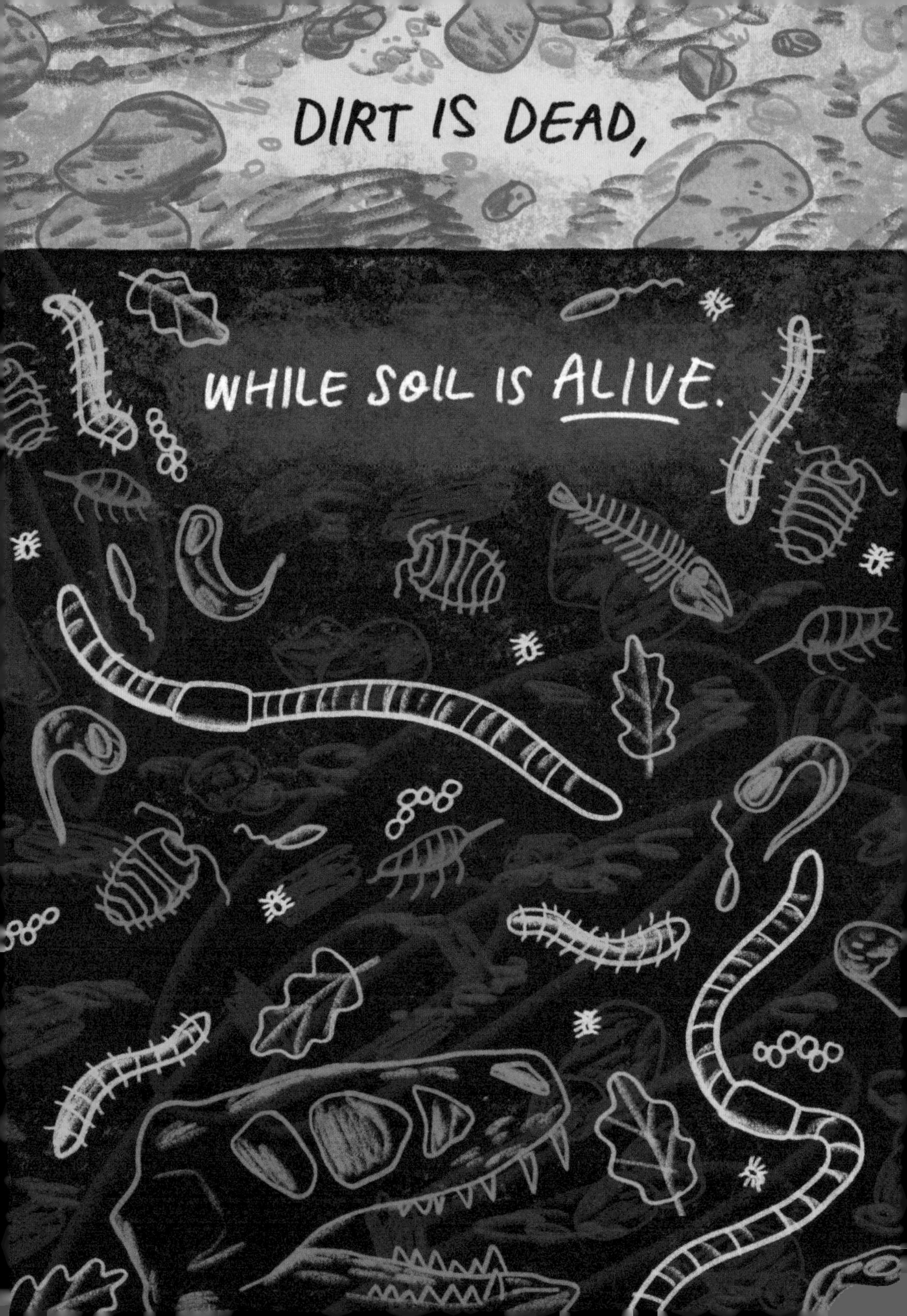
DIRT IS DEAD,
WHILE SOIL IS ALIVE.

BUT WHAT MAKES SOIL SO ALIVE IS THAT IT'S FULL OF DEATH.

STILL WITH ME?

In healthy soil, worms, fungi, bugs, and bacteria help transform the bodies of dead things into vital nutrients. Without all those dead things, soil isn't soil at all. Devoid of that decomposed matter, dirt has nothing to offer a young seedling.

SOIL IS A MIX OF THE LIVING, THE DEAD, AND THE VERY DEAD — AS SOME WISE, OLD GARDENERS ARE WONT TO SAY.

It uses that which
came before . . .

Petroglyph,
c. 3rd millennium, B.C.,
Camuni people

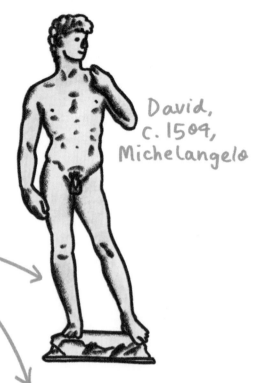

David,
c. 1504,
Michelangelo

Vitruvian Man,
c. 1490,
Leonardo da Vinci

Sketchbook,
present day,
YOU

. . . to create all that
is yet to come.

CREATING HEALTHY SOIL IS A PROCESS, NOT JUST A ONE-TIME DEAL.

This cycle helps sustain every living thing on the planet.

Fungi, like the vibrant pink oyster mushroom, are instrumental in the breaking down of organic matter, transforming it into the necessary nutrients to support new life.

Pleurotus djamor

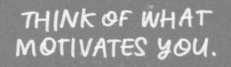

THINK OF WHAT MOTIVATES YOU.

How do you keep this well of inspiration deep and full?

How can you make sure your soil doesn't die and become dirt?

What can you add to your soil to ensure your friendships and other close relationships stay nourished?

CURIOSITY

PASSION

AMBITION

FERTILIZER

IF YOU CAN LEARN TO MAINTAIN AND REPLENISH SUCH RICH, HEALTHY SOIL, YOU STAND TO BENEFIT FROM A LIFETIME OF NOURISHMENT.

HOW TO CULTIVATE NOURISHING SOIL

STEP 1
GATHER THINGS FROM THE PAST

chamaedorea elegans

Dead things—that is to say, things from our past—are a treasure trove of inspiration. They remind us where we've been to better illuminate where we would like to go. Whether good, bad, or downright ugly, we cannot exist today without the past—even if there are some things we would rather forget.

COLLECT SOME THINGS YOU HAVE LEFT BEHIND.

If they are tangible, hold them in your hand.
If not, hold them in your mind.

It might bring up some complicated feelings to reunite
with these things. Perhaps you never fully grieved them
because you never fully admitted they were gone.

PERHAPS YOU EVEN FEEL SHAME.

IT'S OKAY.

Even if you can't bear to look at those things
from the past, they can still be helpful.

THEY ARE A TRIBUTE NOW,
A GIFT TO YOUR FUTURE GROWTH.

THANK THEM FOR
THE EXPERIENCE
THEY PROVIDED,

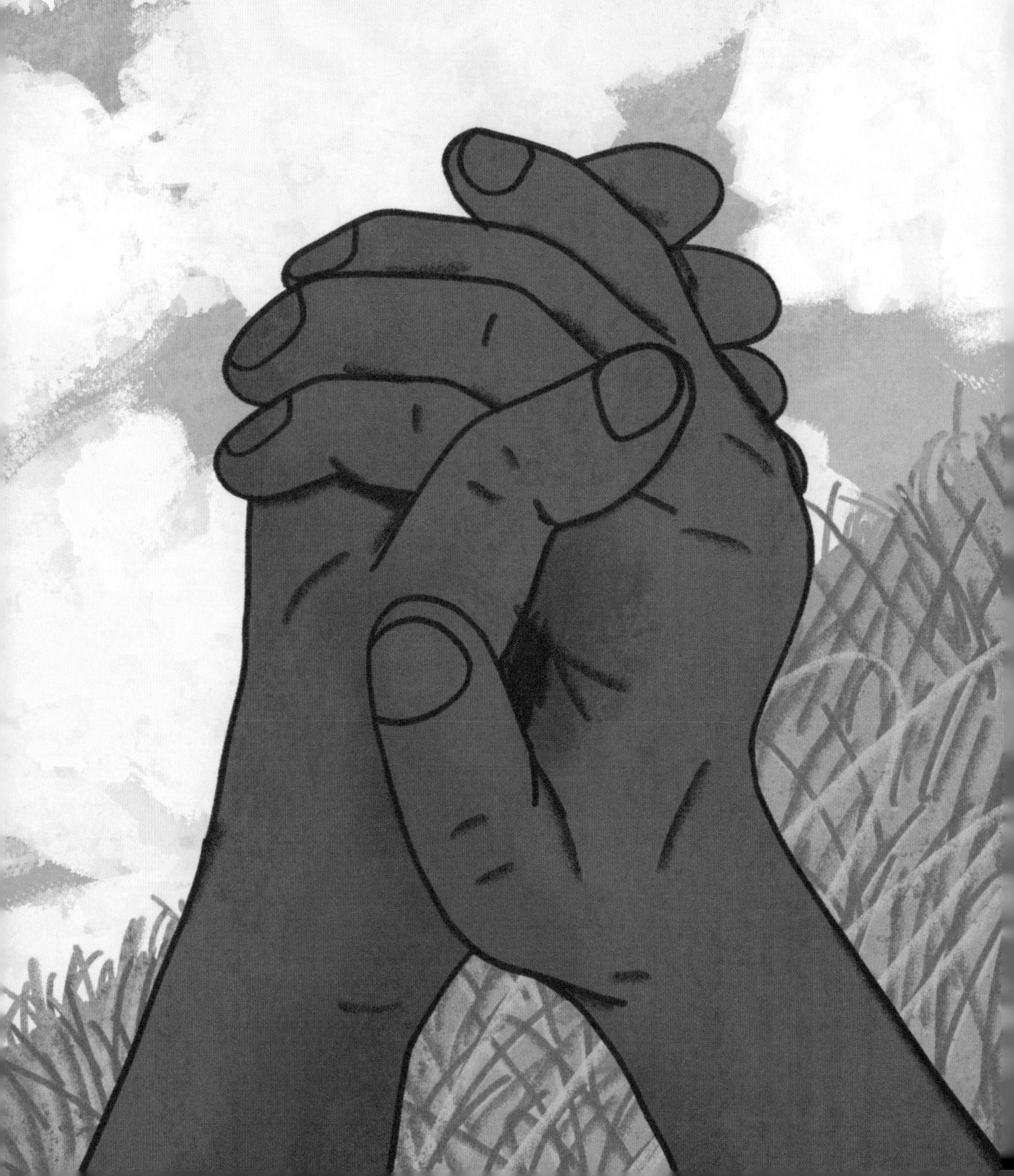

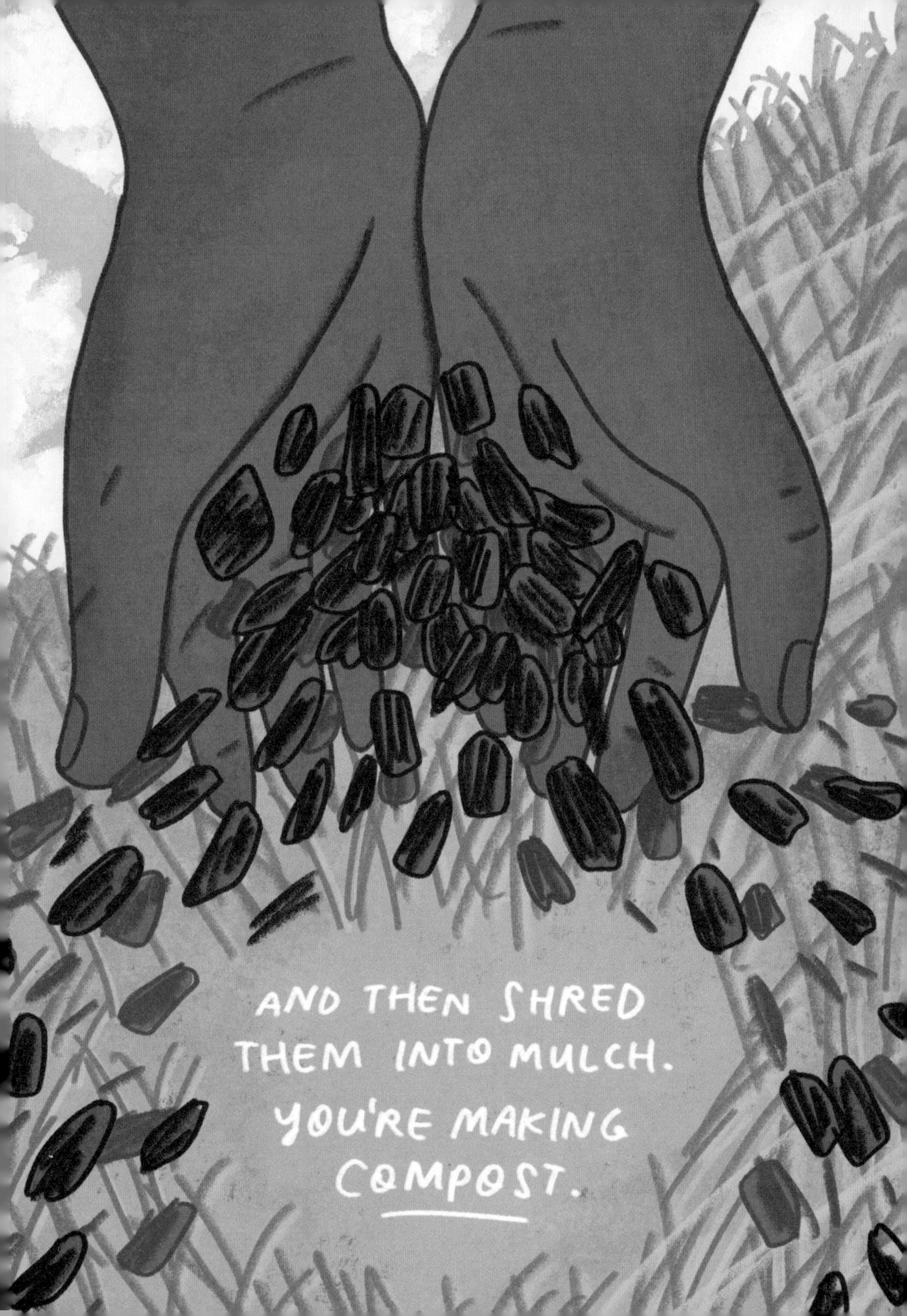
AND THEN SHRED
THEM INTO MULCH.
YOU'RE MAKING
COMPOST.

STEP 2
GATHER THINGS FROM THE PRESENT

The past is important, but here in the present is where new things happen. Look around you. The world is full of things to inspire you today.

a cause you believe in

a stream roaring after a rainstorm

a nerdy documentary

the work of forest ecologist Dr. Suzanne Simard

funny dogs

people waiting in a line

THESE THINGS WILL BECOME PART OF YOUR SOIL, TOO.

Jot them down. Take a photo.
Do whatever you can to remember them.

In the same way you might toss kale stems into
a compost bin, throw these new memories in
with the old. With time they will break down, and
new and old will become indistinguishable.

EVENTUALLY, THE PRESENT WILL BECOME THE PAST.

REPEAT

Now that you have some healthy soil, it must be maintained. As the new things decompose into old and the cycle unfolds anew, it will require new material year after year.

IT'S HARD WORK.

BUT THE LONGER YOU
REPEAT THIS PROCESS—

THE GATHERING

AND THE
LETTING GO—

THE
LONGER
YOUR SOIL
WILL
SUSTAIN
YOU.

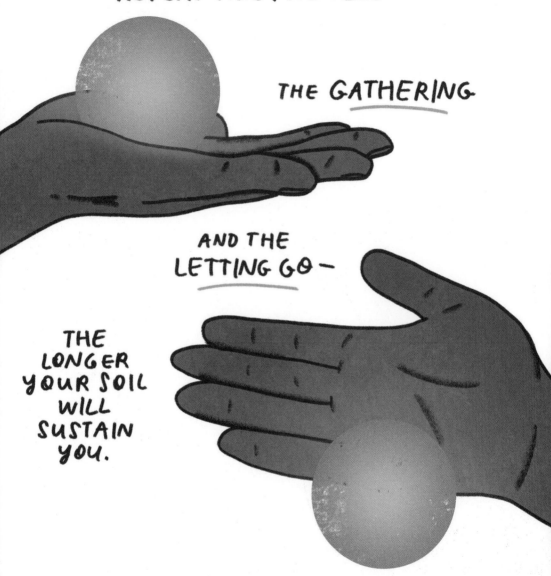

AND THE BETTER YOU'LL
GET AT MAINTAINING IT.

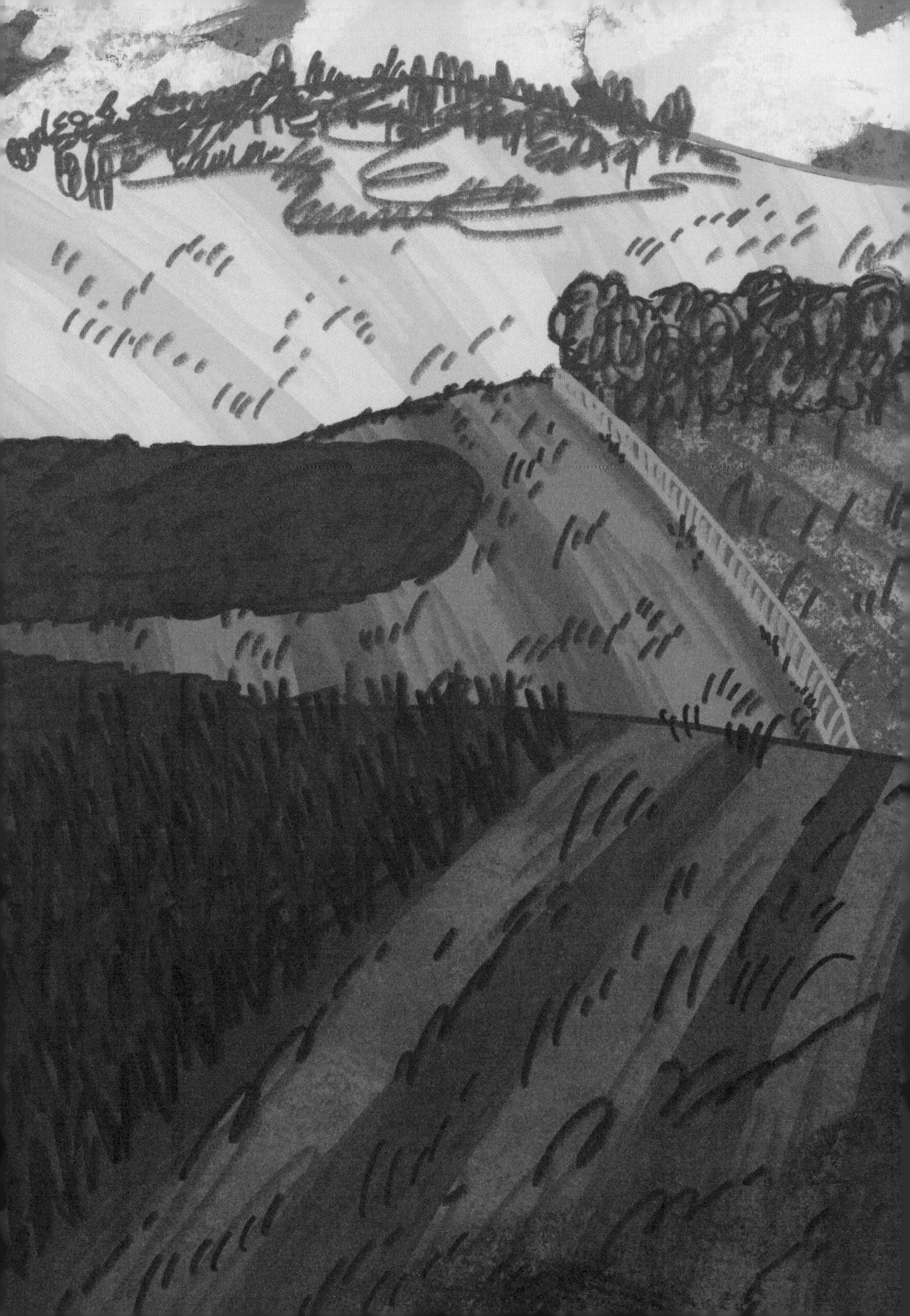

EVENTUALLY IT WILL BECOME SECOND NATURE.

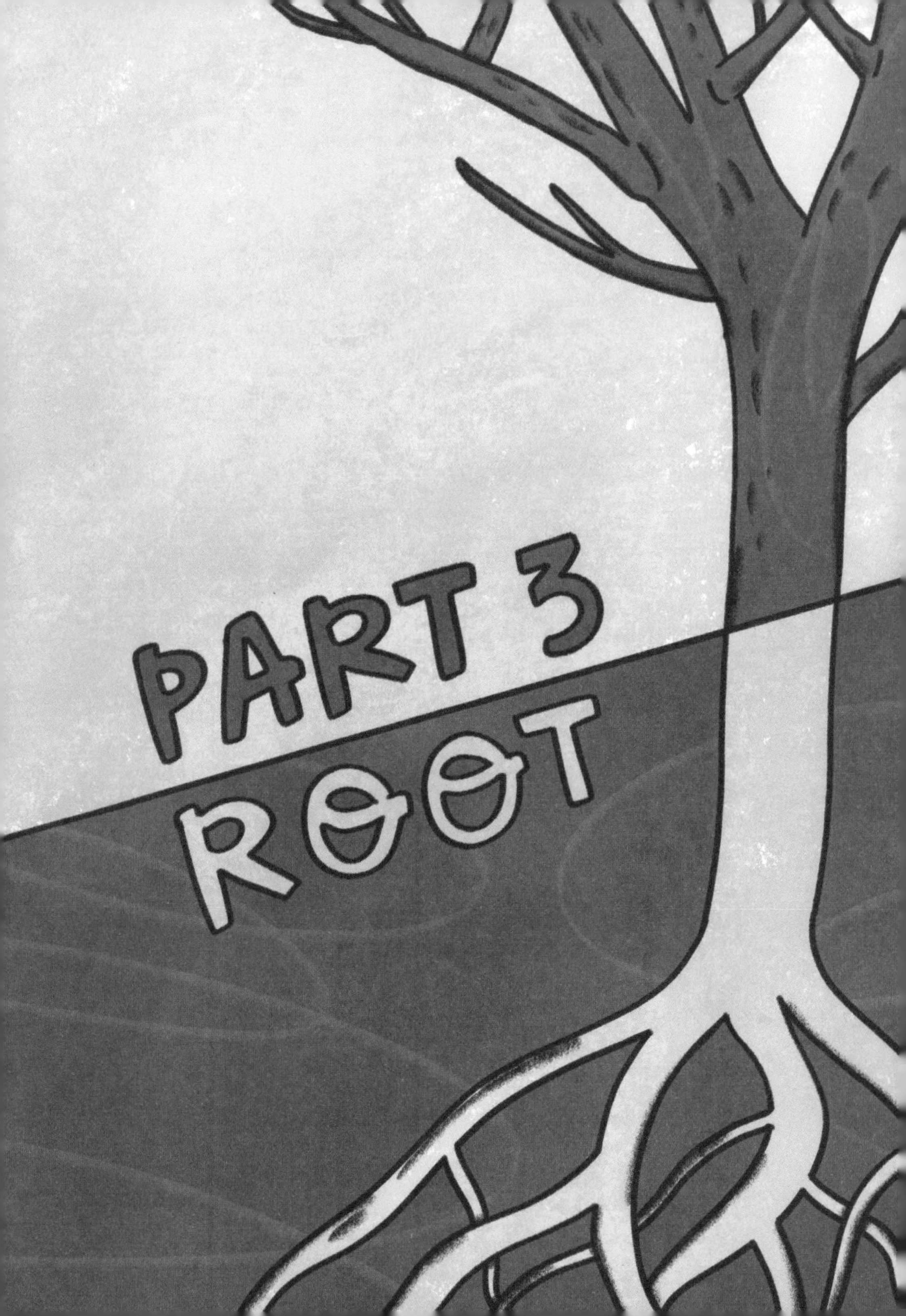
PART 3
ROOT

From where we stand, here on the surface
of the Earth, it's easy to think that
what we see is all there is.

BUT THERE IS OFTEN MORE
THAN MEETS THE EYE.

CONSIDER A TREE:

THE FIRST THING YOU NOTICE IS A BROAD TRUNK,

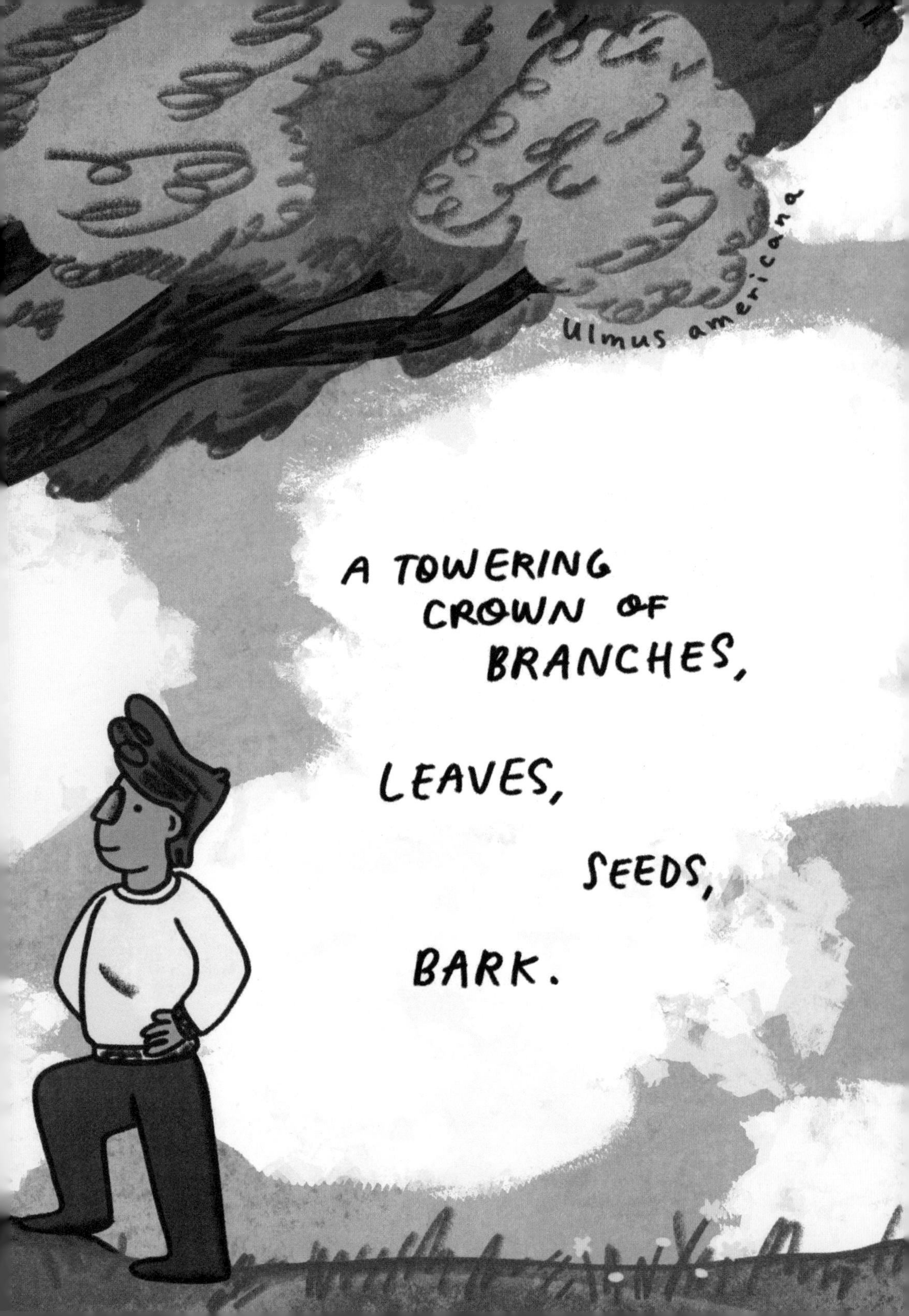
Ulmus americana

A TOWERING
CROWN OF
BRANCHES,

LEAVES,

SEEDS,

BARK.

BUT TO SEE THE WHOLE STORY, YOU'VE GOT TO LOOK...

UNDER

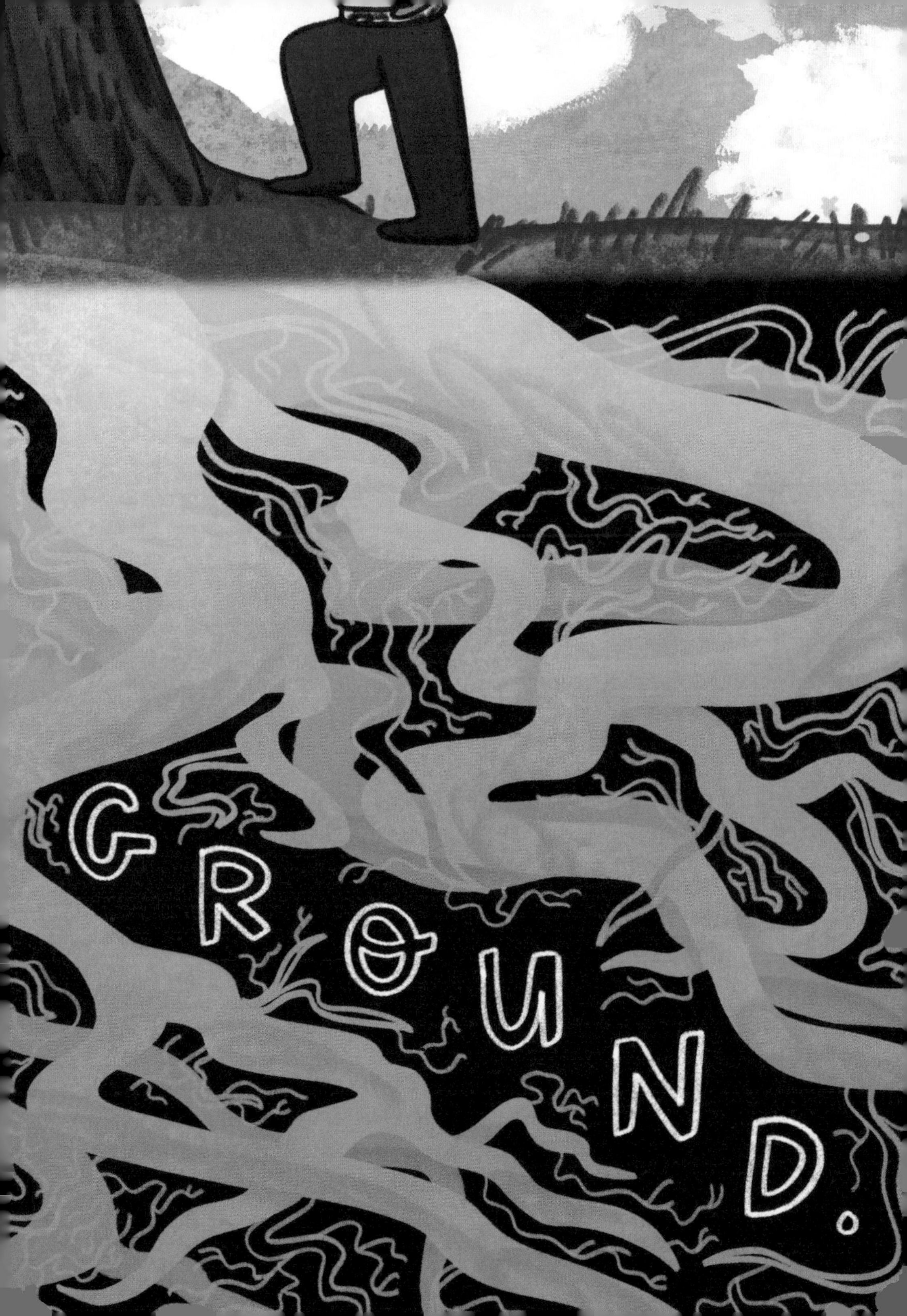
GROUND.

IT'S RARE THAT WE NOTICE ROOTS.

(Unless we've just tripped over one or
if we're repotting a houseplant.)

When the foliage is so bright and abundant, the
roots can feel almost peripheral to what we think
of as the "plant"—even though they usually make
up about a quarter of the plant's total mass.

THOSE ROOTS ARE ITS LIFE SOURCE.

They're the invisible foundations of most of the world's greatest ecosystems.

THINK OF YOUR OWN ROOTS:

Where was your foundation laid? Have you been repotted recently? How deep and wide do your roots go and do they sustain you in the ways you need them to?

Even in the dark, roots don't move blindly. They actively seek out the most nourishing pockets of soil and deftly navigate around obstacles.

TRUE FRIENDS

FAKE FRIENDS

STRESS

CHOSEN FAMILY

JOY

Roots have much more control than we might think.

IT'S ALL INTERTWINED

Beneath the soil, the roots of plants are constantly climbing over and under one another, intertwining and extending in all directions. But in healthy forests, the finest, thinnest roots are also intertwined with something else: fungi. Hairlike fungal filaments called mycelia entangle with the roots to form what's called a mycorrhizal network: an information superhighway, but for plants. Some scientists refer to it as the "wood-wide web."

In this mutualistic relationship, the fungi gain access to a steady supply of sugar and carbon, which they need to survive. The trees receive nutrients, too, but they also gain a much more dynamic benefit: They utilize the dense network of interconnected threads to communicate with their neighbors. Recent studies show that they send signals to other trees, warning them of threats or predators, so the other trees can react accordingly. The trees can also use this network to send nutrients to others in need, like young saplings on the forest floor that don't receive enough sunlight to photosynthesize their own.

It's a massive interkingdom collaboration that helps ensure the well-being of the entire forest.

ROOTS ARE A COMMUNITY.

They are a lifeline, both for themselves
and those around them.

Whether you're alone in a new city or a new
workplace or anywhere you've yet to establish a
space for yourself, the best thing you can do is

FOCUS ON EXTENDING YOUR ROOTS.

HOW TO PUT DOWN ROOTS

ROOTS CAN SERVE DIFFERENT PURPOSES DEPENDING ON THE NEEDS OF THE PLANT.

They grow where they can be most useful, whether it's bringing nourishment to a would-be flower or anchoring an olive tree to the side of a cliff. It's important that you build the roots you need for what you want to accomplish.

Olea europaea

STEP 1
FEEL IT OUT

Starting from scratch is hard, but from the moment
a plant's first root starts diving down out of its seed,
it is beginning the process of looking for its home.

IT TWISTS,
WINDING
ITS WAY
DOWN
THROUGH
THE DIRT
SEEKING
NOURISH-
MENT.

IT DOES
THIS BY
FEELING.
IT IS
DRAWN
TOWARD
THE THINGS
THAT WILL
SERVE IT.

WHAT WILL SERVE YOU?

STEP 2
TAKE UP SPACE

ONCE YOU'VE
ESTABLISHED
WHERE
YOU'D LIKE
TO SEND
YOUR
ROOTS, IT'S
TIME TO
EXPAND.

Let one root become two and two become four
and four become eight and on and on and on.

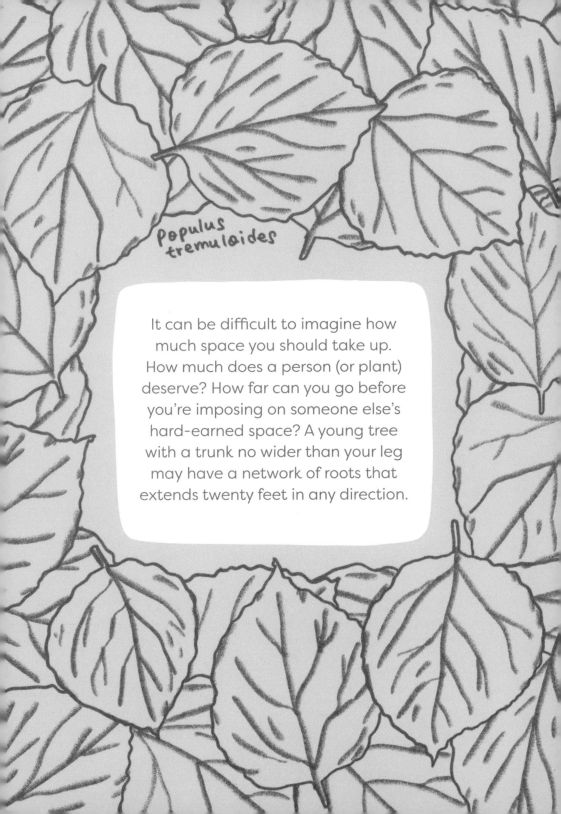

populus
tremuloides

It can be difficult to imagine how much space you should take up. How much does a person (or plant) deserve? How far can you go before you're imposing on someone else's hard-earned space? A young tree with a trunk no wider than your leg may have a network of roots that extends twenty feet in any direction.

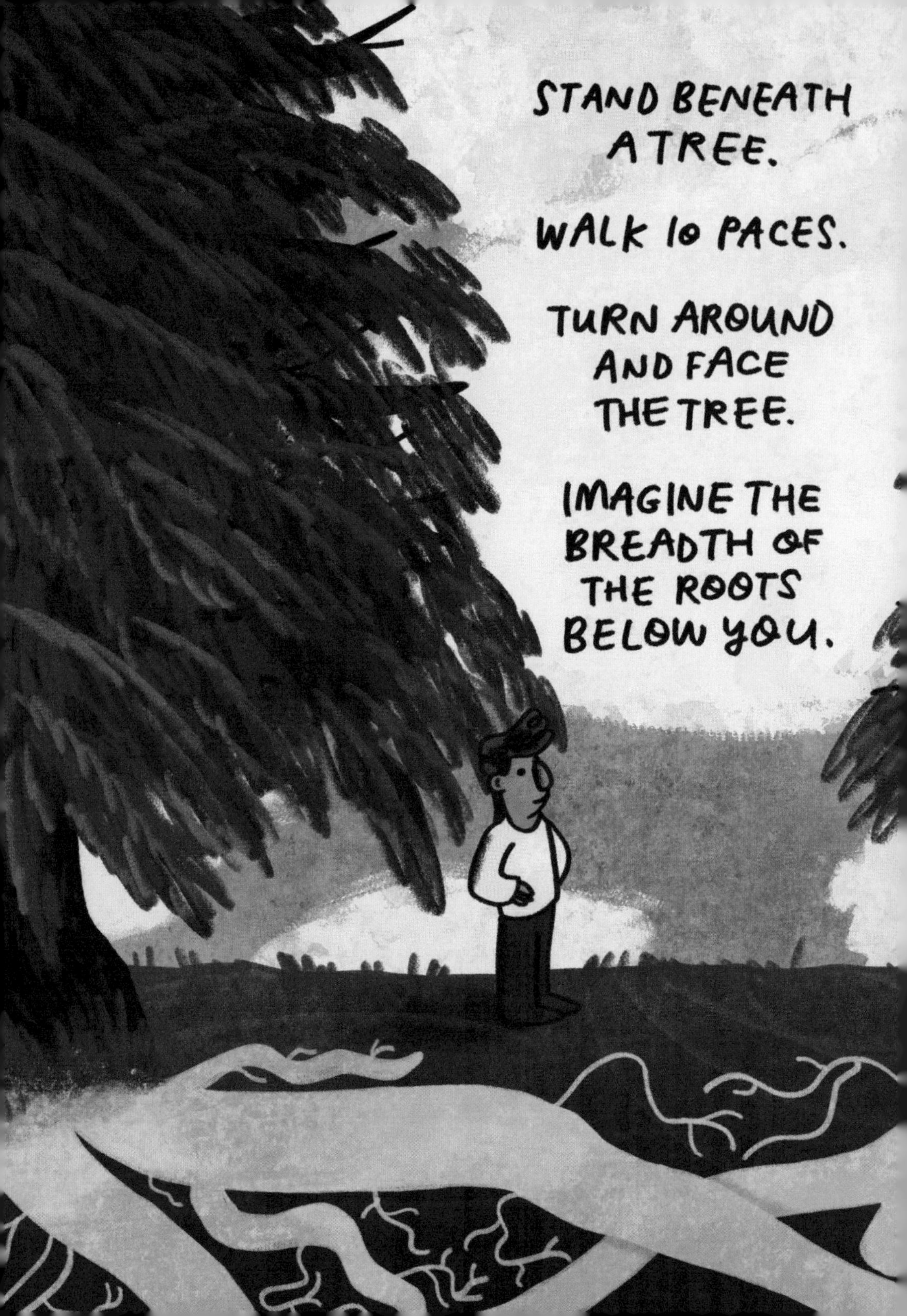
STAND BENEATH A TREE.
WALK 10 PACES.
TURN AROUND AND FACE THE TREE.
IMAGINE THE BREADTH OF THE ROOTS BELOW YOU.

Tsuga
canadensis

THINK OF HOW VAST YOUR OWN ROOTS
CAN BE, AND HOW THEY INTERTWINE
WITH THOSE AROUND THEM.

MAKE ACQUAINTANCES

Your roots are powerful—and they are enough for you to survive. But a forest thrives on the collaboration of hundreds (thousands!) of interconnected species. The individuals benefit because they work as a whole.

TRY GETTING INVOLVED WITH YOUR COMMUNITY

Attend a city council meeting

Join a book club

Volunteer with a local nonprofit

Take a mushroom foraging class

REMEMBER THAT WHILE YOU MAY BE S<u>MALL</u>, YOUR ROOTS ARE ALLOWED TO BE <u>WIDE</u>.

The more they cross and tangle and loop through other roots, the stronger you all will be.

TRY AND STAY A WHILE

IT IS TEMPTING TO ALWAYS BE ON THE MOVE.

And sometimes it's necessary to get out,
whether to escape a bad situation or to avoid
becoming waterlogged and rotting in a pot
that's become too small. But if your roots appear
to be spreading, and if it feels good . . .

TRY STICKING AROUND FOR A BIT.

**SEE HOW
IT _FEELS_.**

YOU MAY BE SURPRISED
TO FIND YOURSELF A PART
OF SOMETHING BIGGER.

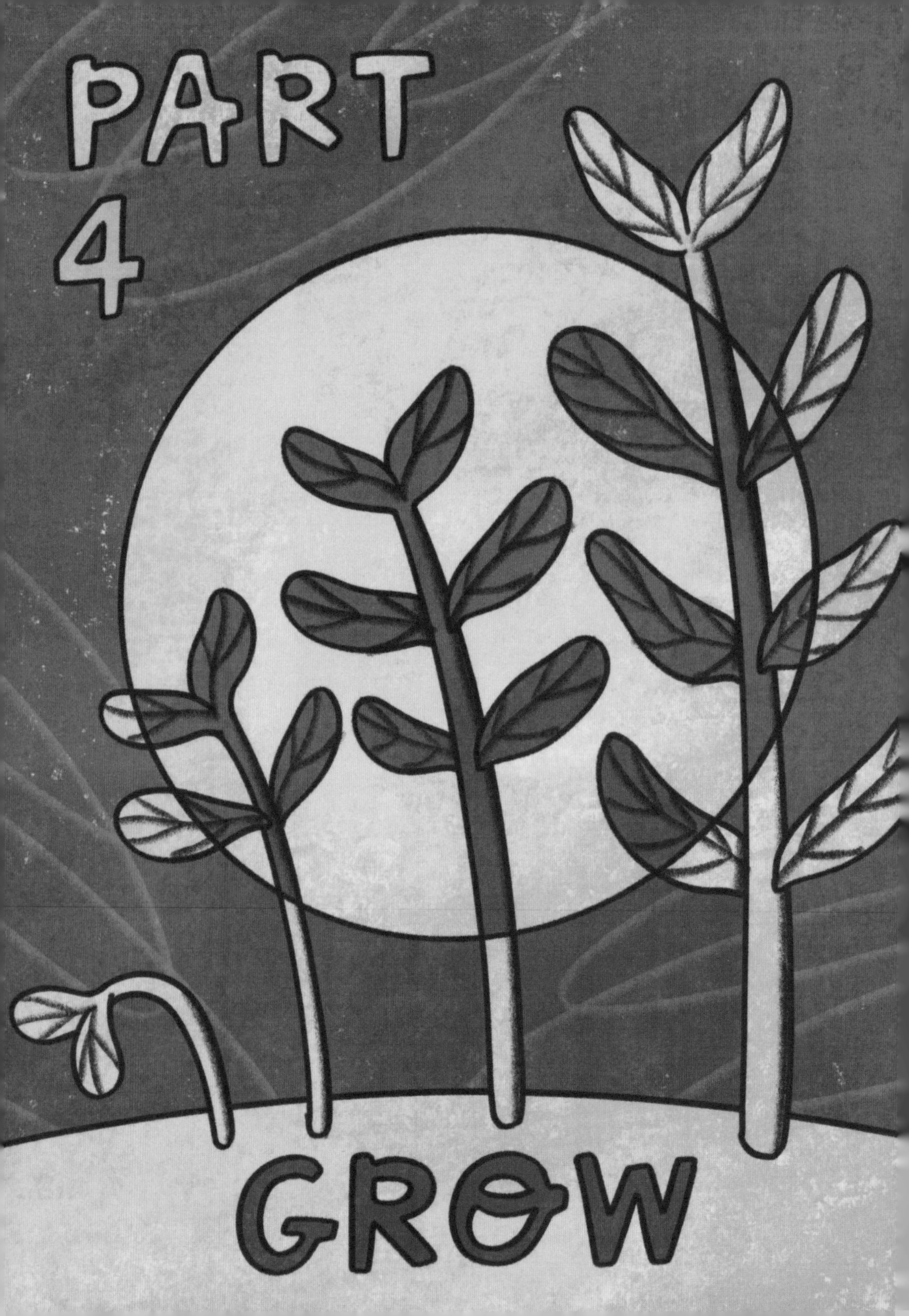
PART 4
GROW

GROWTH TAKES MANY FORMS.

Growth can be shapely and neat or wild
and unwieldy. It can be remarkably quick
or it can take a very long time.

Ficus
benghalensis

Pelargoneum
graveolens

WHATEVER ITS SHAPE AND SIZE, GROWTH IS NEVER WITHOUT PURPOSE.

Each plant has a unique road map
for how it grows, whether it's by
branches or vines, stalks or shoots.

SPRUCE   WILLOW   PALM   LINDEN

BAOBAB   POPLAR   OAK   PINE

A plant knows intrinsically what shape to
take for the work it needs to do: If it's what
comes naturally, it's probably right.

AND IT ALL BEGINS WITH THE SUN.

LONG STORY SHORT, PLANTS USE SUNLIGHT TO GROW.

CARBON DIOXIDE

WATER

GLUCOSE

OXYGEN

Epipremnum aureum

The long story is that plants use cellular structures called chloroplasts to undergo photosynthesis, which allows them to capture the energy from sunlight and use it to convert water and carbon dioxide into oxygen and glucose, respectively. Some of this glucose is used as food for the plant, while the rest is converted into cellulose, which makes up more cells. That's growth!

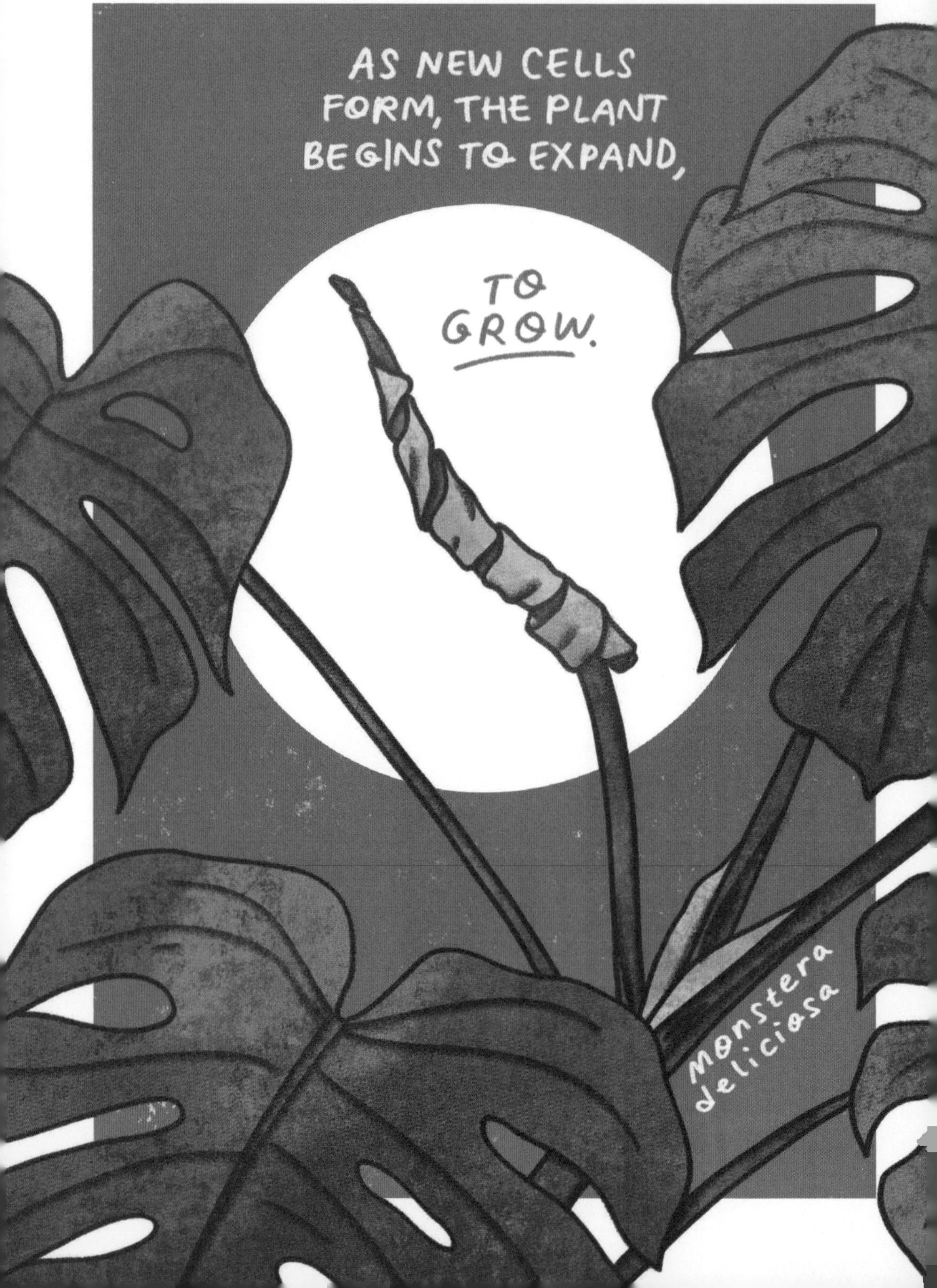
AS NEW CELLS FORM, THE PLANT BEGINS TO EXPAND,
TO GROW.
Monstera deliciosa

It may appear to create its stems and leaves and tendrils
out of thin air, but it isn't magic—it is a *transformation*.

THE STUFF OF GROWTH IS
EVERYWHERE, AND IT IS ALWAYS
AVAILABLE FOR THE TAKING.

BUT SUNLIGHT AND WATER ARE SELDOM ALL THAT'S REQUIRED TO THRIVE: A SEED NEEDS NOURISHMENT.

This is the difference between survival and abundance.
Thankfully lots of things can be nourishing:

Phosphorous

Nitrogen

Potassium

Yoga

French fries

Long talks with a friend over a good meal

What makes one plant thrive might stunt the growth of another. Too much of one thing and you might find yourself sluggish and unmotivated. (I'm looking at you, French fries.)

Leafy greens like cabbage and kale explode with life if the soil is rich in nitrogen. But a tomato plant in the same soil might end up looking like a big green bush with no fruit to speak of.

THE REAL TRICK IS FIGURING OUT WHAT WORKS BEST FOR you.

HOW TO NOURISH YOUR BEST GROWTH

STEP 1

IDENTIFY WHAT YOU WANT YOUR GROWTH TO LOOK LIKE

Do you want to spread like strawberries or climb like peas? Are you going to put forth dozens of fiery hot peppers or produce one glorious head of cabbage?

All are valid options, but the best way to
see it through is to start off with a goal.

Strelitzia
reginae

ASK YOURSELF:
HOW DO I HOPE TO GROW?
WHAT DO I WANT TO ACHIEVE?

A BRIEF NOTE ON JEALOUSY

Occasionally it can feel like someone else is growing in exactly the way we are hoping to—and how easy and effortless it looks! It's helpful to remember, though, that things are not always as they seem at first glance. It usually requires a certain amount of experience to appear so effortless. Snap peas, for example, are easy to grow, but without a trellis or fence to climb, the vines will flounder on the ground, tangling themselves into knots. A little bit of knowledge can make all the difference.

Comparing our own growth to the growth of others is a sure-fire way to feel bad about our progress. But that jealousy you're stewing in? It means two things: First, that you're passionate about something. We don't feel jealousy over things we don't care about. And second, that a model exists in the world for what your own success could look like. Jealousy is a stagnating force though. It sits and rots, and it inhibits growth. Remember that someone else's growth doesn't mean there isn't room for yours. Our goal might be the same, but the individual paths we each take to get there are one of a kind.

Let jealousy
be a guide—

an opportunity to clarify and hone your vision.

Take notes. Gather knowledge. Ask questions (politely).

You may even make a friend along the way.

FIGURE OUT WHAT NOURISHES YOU

JADE PLANT	MARSH FERN	SNAKE PLANT
Crassula argentea	Thelypteris palustris	Sansevieria zeylanica

DIRECT SUN, FULL BLAST	SHADE, CONSTANT HUMIDITY	WILL TAKE WHATEVER IT CAN GET

Different plants have different needs, so before you can grow in your desired direction, you have to figure out what kind of plant you are: Are you a hardy desert cactus or a delicate tropical orchid? A potted begonia or a wild wisteria?

UNFORTUNATELY, AN
INTERNET QUIZ CANNOT
TELL YOU THIS.

YOU'RE A SAGUARO CACTUS!

Carnegiea gigantea

You're 40 feet tall, covered
in spines, and filled with like
1,500 gallons of water! Cool!
You're also the only species in
your genus, so you'll probably
be alone forever. Womp womp.

IT WILL REQUIRE
SOME EXPERIMENTATION.

MAKE A LIST OF WHAT GIVES YOU LIFE.

IF NOTHING COMES TO MIND, IMAGINE SOME THINGS THAT MIGHT GIVE YOU LIFE IF YOU WERE TO TRY THEM. THEN TRY THEM.

DO A 15-MINUTE MEDITATION EVERY MORNING FOR A WEEK.

SWIM SOME LAPS AT YOUR LOCAL POOL. (OR JUST FLOAT.)

START A MONTHLY ACCOUNTABILITY CHECK-IN WITH A FRIEND.

SWITCH FROM COFFEE IN
THE MORNING TO TEA.

SWITCH FROM
TEA TO
BUBBLE TEA???

TRY
JOURNALING
REGULARLY.

DO THAT THING YOU
KEEP THINKING
ABOUT DOING BUT
HAVEN'T DONE YET.

(YOU KNOW
THE ONE.)

WHATEVER YOU DO, THE MOST IMPORTANT THING IS THAT YOU DON'T STOP TRYING THINGS!

Once you've tried a thing, take stock of how it made you feel. Was it good? Was it bad? Did it make you feel a little intimidated at first but maybe possibly in an exciting way that makes you want to try again?

GOOD. KEEP EXPLORING.

Eventually you'll find the right mix of things that work for you. (And if one stops working, switch it up again!)

LET IT HAPPEN

This one sounds obvious, but once you've figured out what sends you flying, you've got to let it do its job.

Growth requires patience, especially if you're starting from something as small as a seed.

BUT ONCE YOU HIT YOUR STRIDE, THERE'S NO STOPPING YOUR GROWTH.

Make a routine and fill it with the things that nourish you.

Stick with it.

Give it a month, two months, six months.

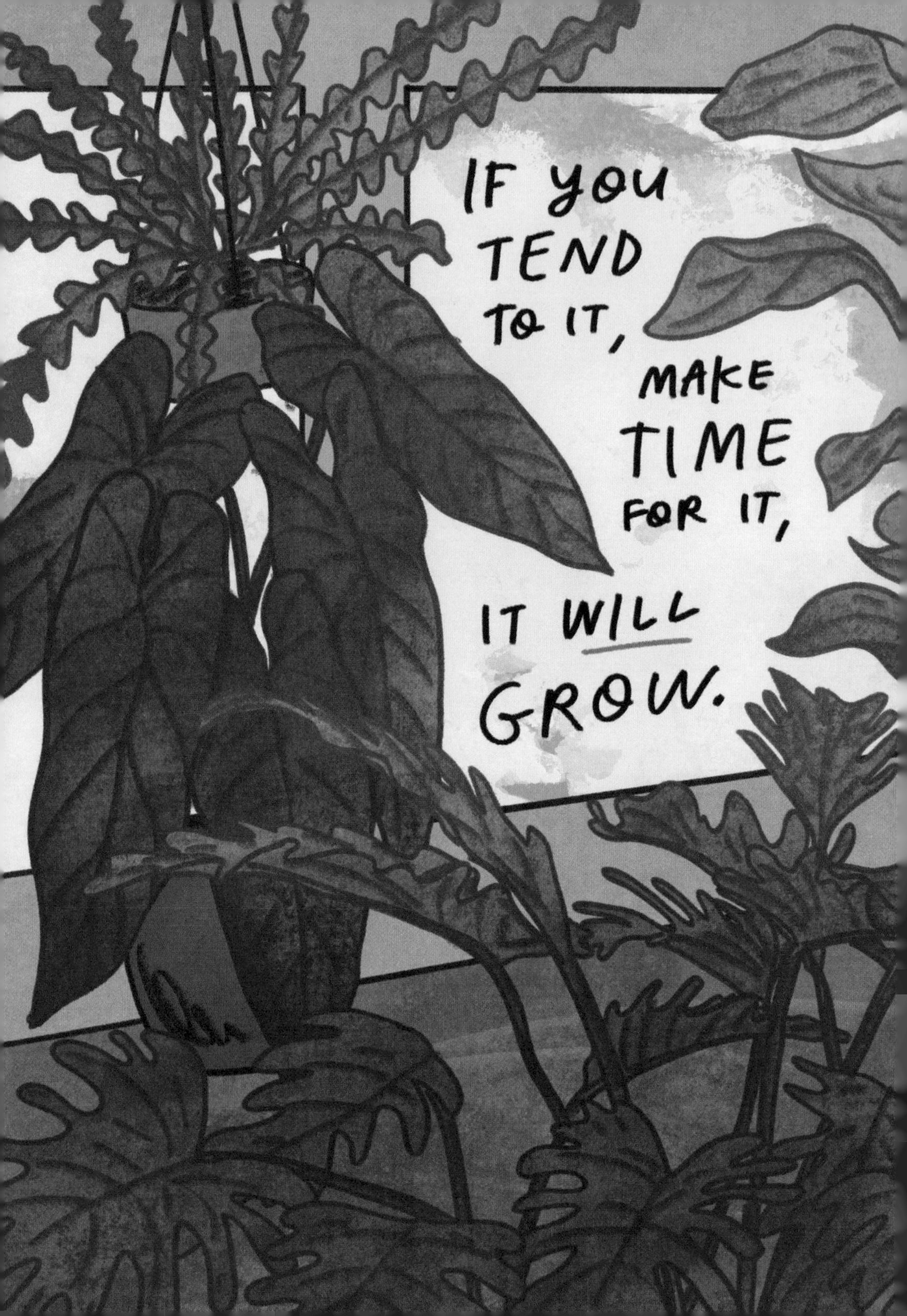
IF YOU
TEND
TO IT,
MAKE
TIME
FOR IT,
IT WILL
GROW.

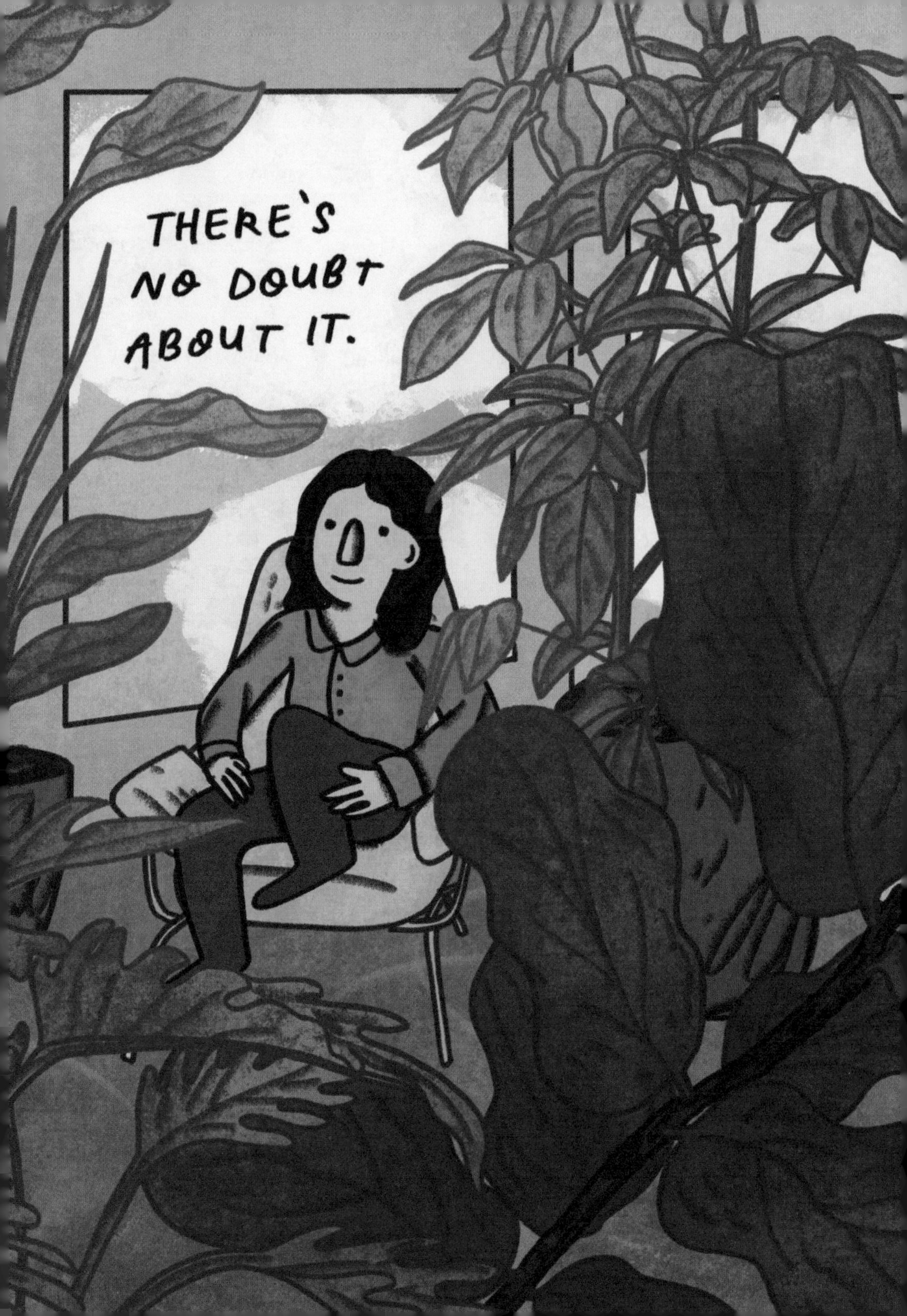
THERE'S NO DOUBT ABOUT IT.

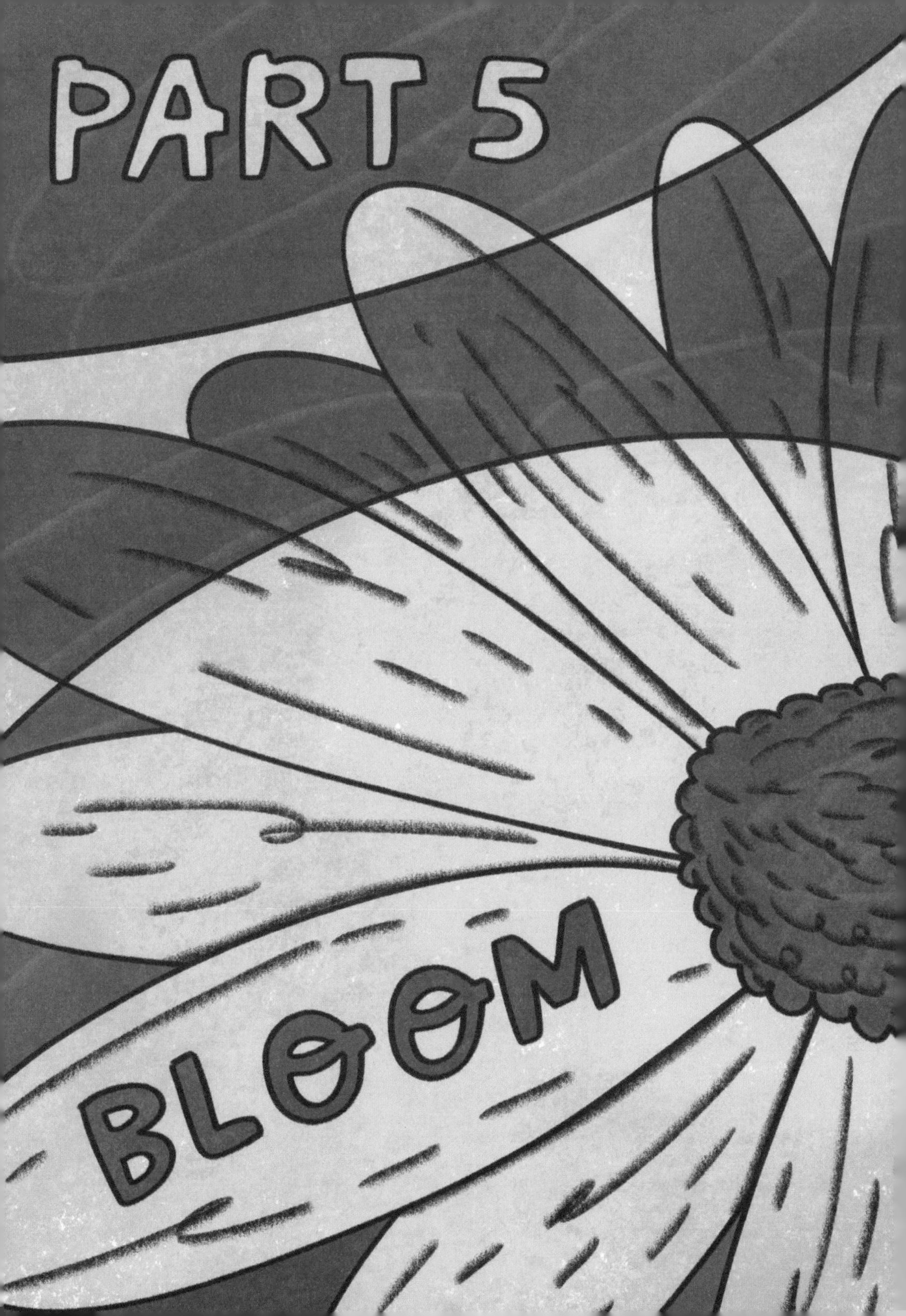
PART 5
BLOOM

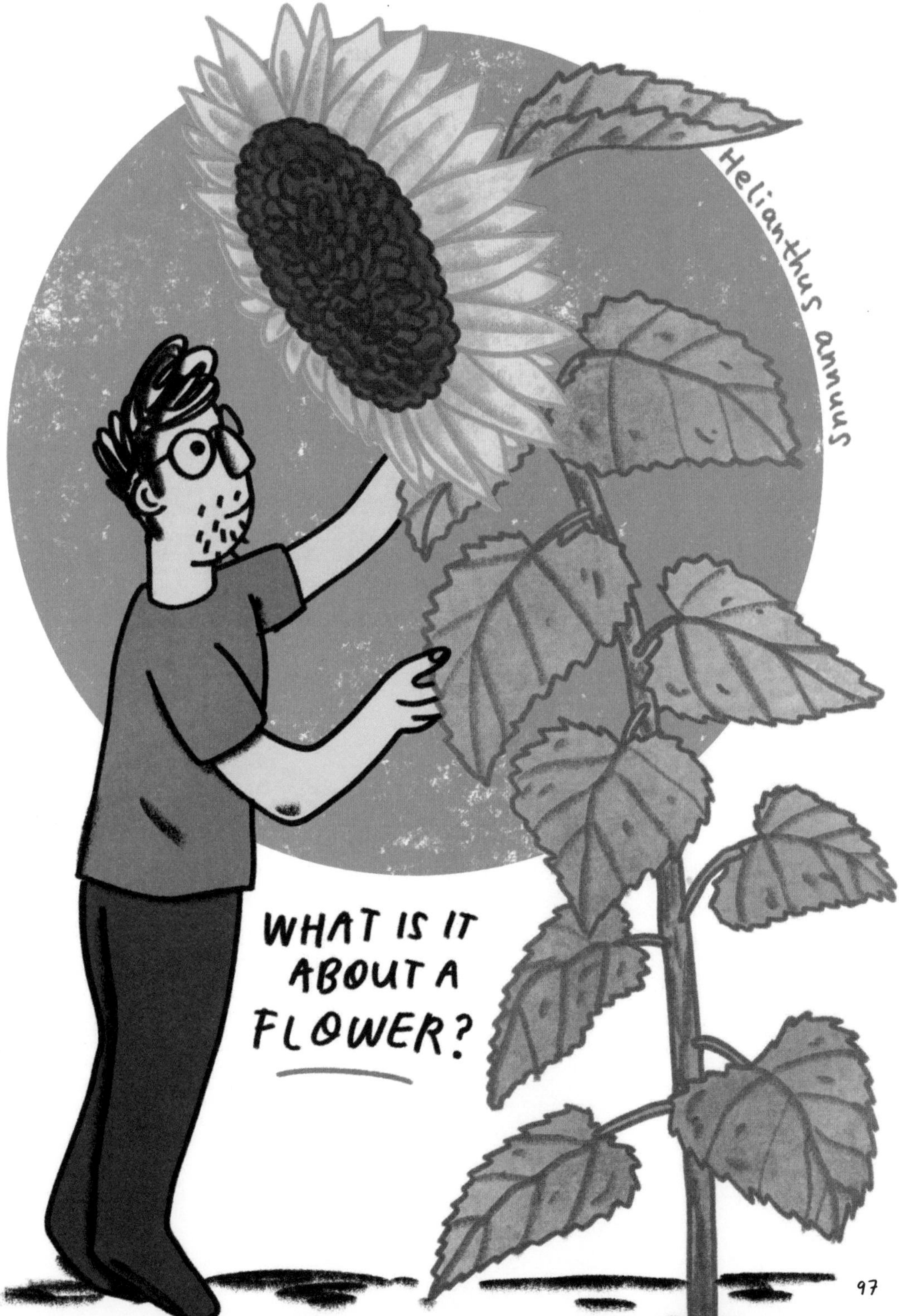
Helianthus annuus
WHAT IS IT ABOUT A FLOWER?

Cosmos bipinnatus

The flower's main purpose, of course, is to aid in the fertilizing of its seeds: to reproduce.

BUT JUST LOOK AT IT!
IS IT THE COLOR?
THE SACRED GEOMETRY?
Dahlia pinnata
THE TANTALIZING SCENT OR THE UNDULATING RIPPLES OF THE PETALS?
OR THE WAY IT ALL BECOMES LUMINOUS IN THE LIGHT OF A RAINY AFTERNOON?

HOWEVER THEY GO ABOUT IT, FLOWERS BECKON TO US.

papaver nudicaule

A BLOOM IS DESIGNED TO ATTRACT, TO DRAW IN ALL THOSÉ WHO WOULD LAZ EYES ON IT—HUMANS, BUGS, AND BIRDS ALIKE.

A FLOWER IS A CELEBRATION!

It's a goal achieved, a dream fully realized.

It is the epitome of accomplishment, standing tall for all to see.

Allium aflatunense

OOOOOOHH

AHHHHHHH

There's no wonder we wrap them in
heaping bouquets to give as gifts for special
occasions or to commemorate success.

THEY ARE A REMINDER OF
WHAT IS POSSIBLE WHEN THE RIGHT
CIRCUMSTANCES ALIGN.

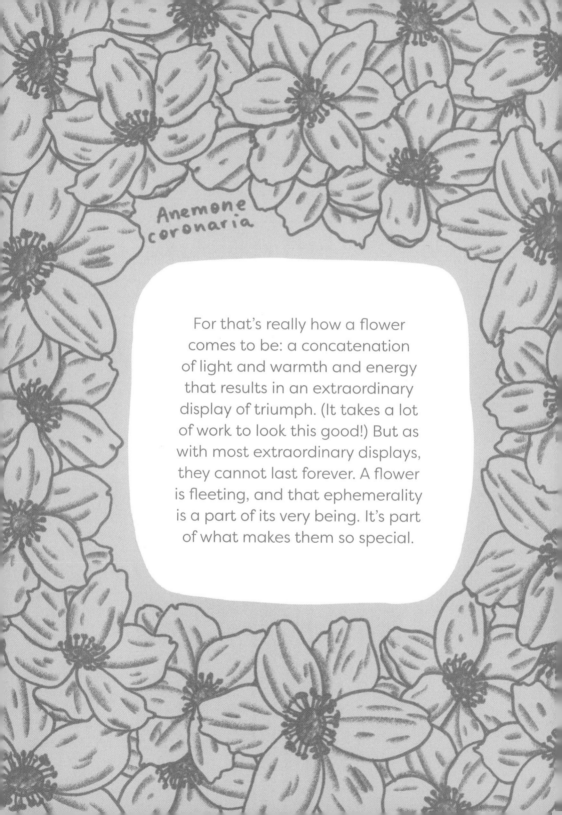

Anemone
coronaria

For that's really how a flower comes to be: a concatenation of light and warmth and energy that results in an extraordinary display of triumph. (It takes a lot of work to look this good!) But as with most extraordinary displays, they cannot last forever. A flower is fleeting, and that ephemerality is a part of its very being. It's part of what makes them so special.

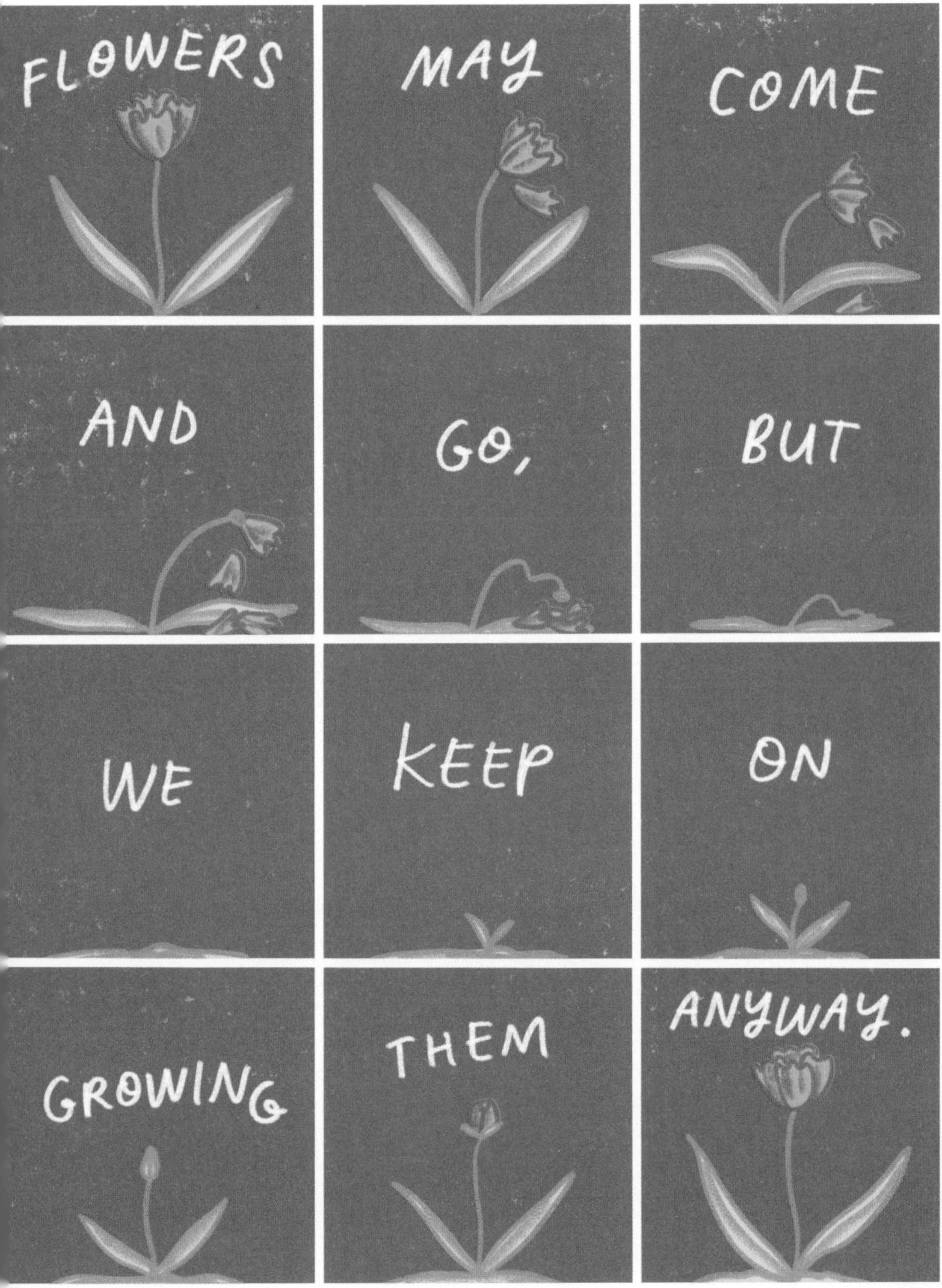
FLOWERS
MAY
COME
AND
GO,
BUT
WE
KEEP
ON
GROWING
THEM
ANYWAY.

HOW TO BLOOM TRIUMPHANTLY

STEP 1
LAY YOUR FOUNDATIONS

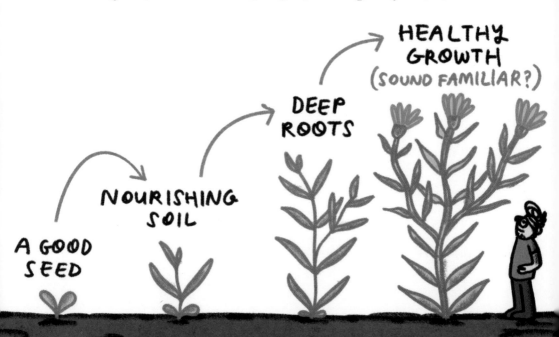

HEALTHY GROWTH
(SOUND FAMILIAR?)

DEEP ROOTS

NOURISHING SOIL

A GOOD SEED

It would be wonderful if flowers could just
pop out of the ground whenever we wanted.
(And sometimes they do!)

BUT IT USUALLY TAKES A LITTLE EFFORT.

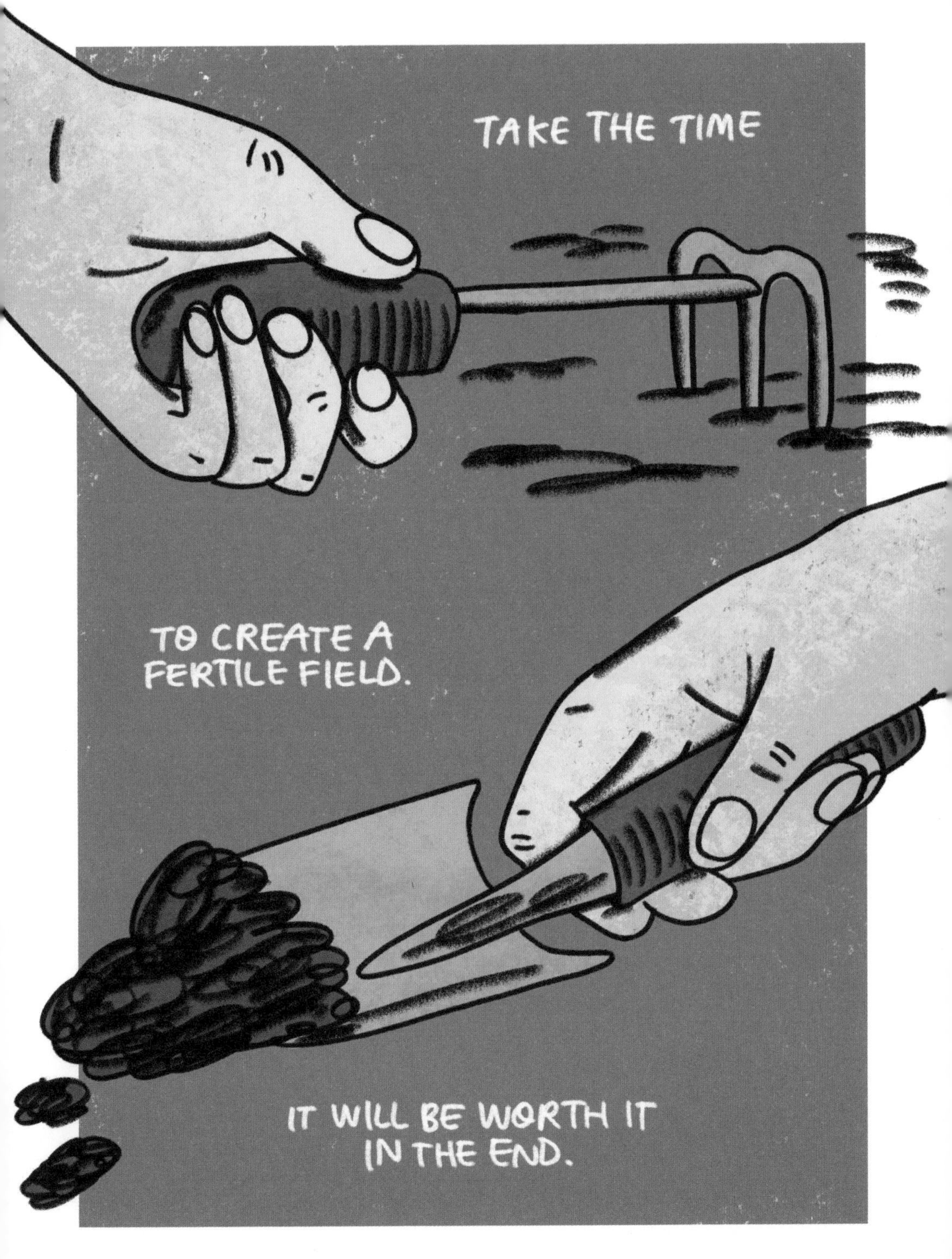
TAKE THE TIME
TO CREATE A FERTILE FIELD.
IT WILL BE WORTH IT IN THE END.

STEP 2
MANAGE YOUR EXPECTATIONS

It takes a lot of work to grow a flower from seed, and there can be a lot of pressure to get it "right."

You spend so much time tending to something, you come to expect a certain result by the time the blooms come around.

You've seen other gardens unfold, watched other flowers in faraway meadows sway in the breeze. Maybe you've felt some jealousy.

BUT WHEN YOUR OWN BLOOMING FINALLY HAPPENS, TRY NOT TO COMPARE IT TO WHAT YOU'VE SEEN BEFORE.

LOOK CLOSELY AT WHAT'S IN FRONT OF YOU.

FOLLOW THE CONTOURS OF ITS PETALS, COUNT THEIR NUMBER, NOTICE THE SUBTLE VARIATIONS IN COLOR. FEEL HOW SOFT OR COARSE THEY ARE AGAINST YOUR SKIN.

paeonia officinalis

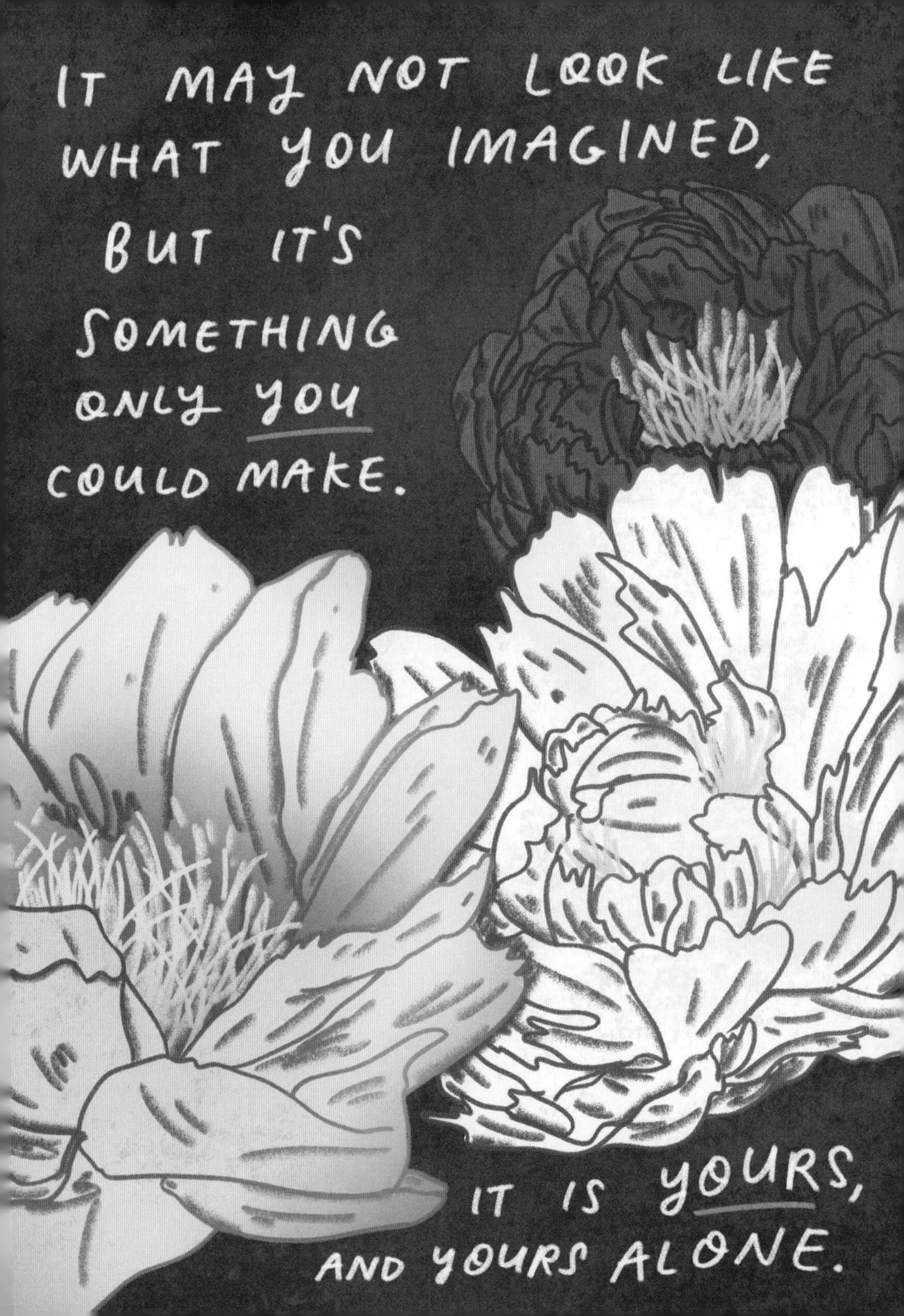
IT MAY NOT LOOK LIKE
WHAT YOU IMAGINED,
BUT IT'S
SOMETHING
ONLY YOU
COULD MAKE.
IT IS YOURS,
AND YOURS ALONE.

STEP 3
CELEBRATE

TAKE A MOMENT AND APPRECIATE WHAT YOU'VE DONE!!!

Once you've bloomed, it can be tempting to pick apart your own success, to belittle it, or to drift back into old, unsatisfying habits. But don't do that!!! You worked hard for these flowers! You had a vision and here it is!!! In real life!!! Gather your loved ones and have some fun with it. Remember:

YOU EARNED THIS.

COMMEMORATE

It's remarkable how long we can work
on something and how relatively quickly
the bliss of achievement can fade.

Echinacea purpurea

BUT YOU BLOOMED ONCE ALREADY;
YOU'VE GOT MORE IN YOU STILL.

Let your earlier blooms inspire you for what's yet to come. Cut a few stems and arrange them in a vase. Every achievement counts, no matter how modest the negotiation or how humble the pie. A tiny flower in an even tinier vase will appear enormous.

AS MORE BLOOMS COME, KEEP HOLDING ON TO THEM.

FILL EVERY SURFACE OF YOUR HOME WITH THESE MEMENTOS OF YOUR BLOOMING,

SO YOU MAY NEVER FORGET WHAT GREAT THINGS YOU ARE CAPABLE OF.

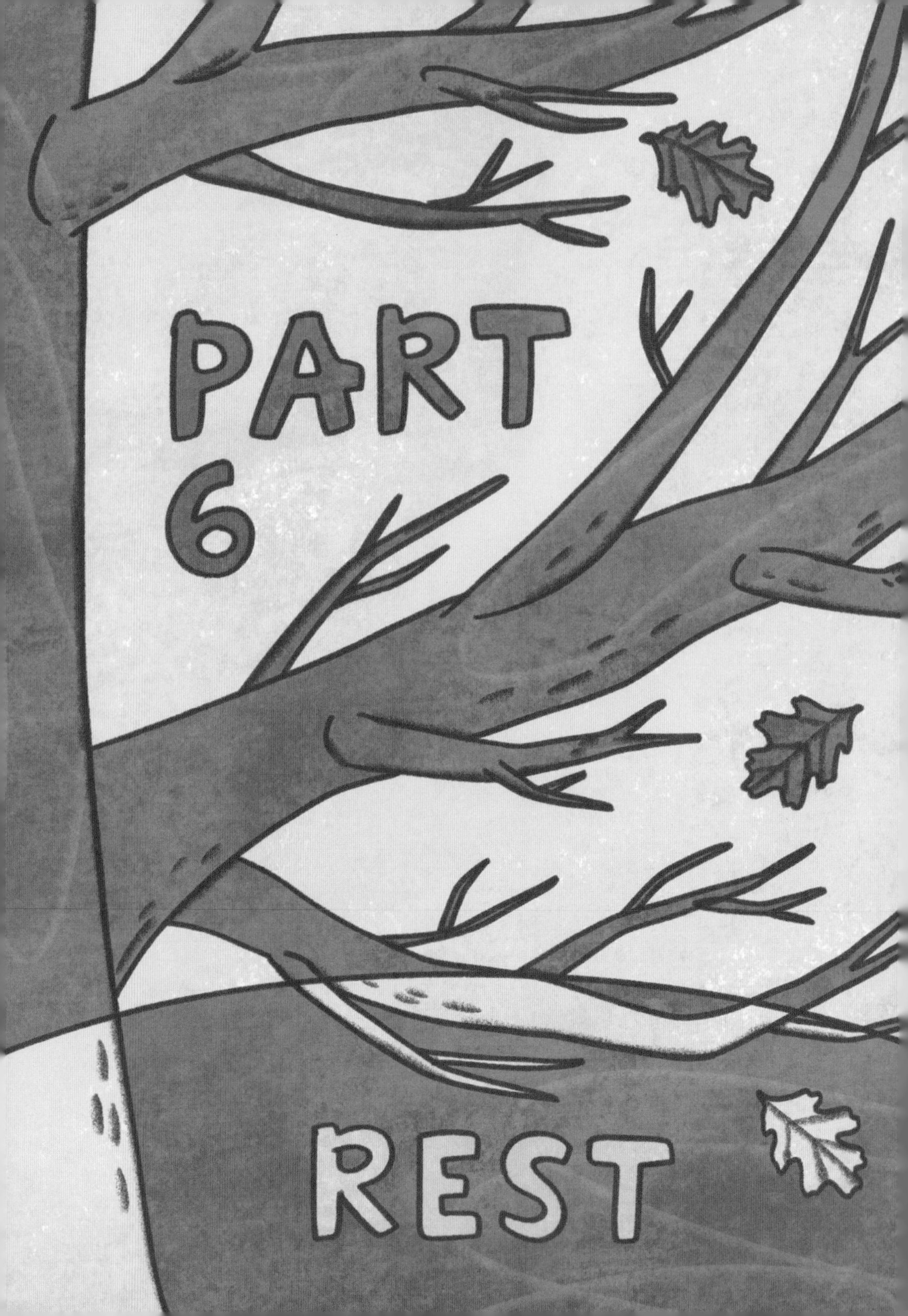
PART 6
REST

Plants aren't always living
in a time of abundance.

MOST

EXPERIENCE

THEIR

LIVES

IN

CYCLES.

SPRING BRINGS RENEWAL,

Malus domestica

SUMMER BRINGS GROWTH,

AND AUTUMN BRINGS THE HARVEST.

But what about winter? Even evergreens, which appear unchanged throughout the frigid months, are entering a new phase.

THEY'RE RESTING.

Plants go dormant in anticipation of hard times—times
when they know the resources they need will be scarce,
be it warmth, sunlight, or water. They intuitively understand
what they need to thrive and when it's best to

HUNKER DOWN AND RIDE OUT THE STORM.

Going dormant isn't just a coping mechanism to get through a tough time; it's also a critical conservation of resources for the work still to come. That little seed has come a long way by now, and even a short rest can help ensure its future growth is greater than ever before.

Magnolia stellata

Many flowering trees have already started to create their spring buds by the time winter's cold dark rolls around. They know it's coming and they plan for it.

When trees shed their leaves, or when perennial plants like peonies wither and die back, they're keeping the nutrients they made all summer safely stored below ground in their roots. From our perspective, they appear dead.

BUT THEY'RE STILL PAYING ATTENTION.

They're noticing the changes in temperature, tracking the increasing sunlight, and reading the signs of spring.

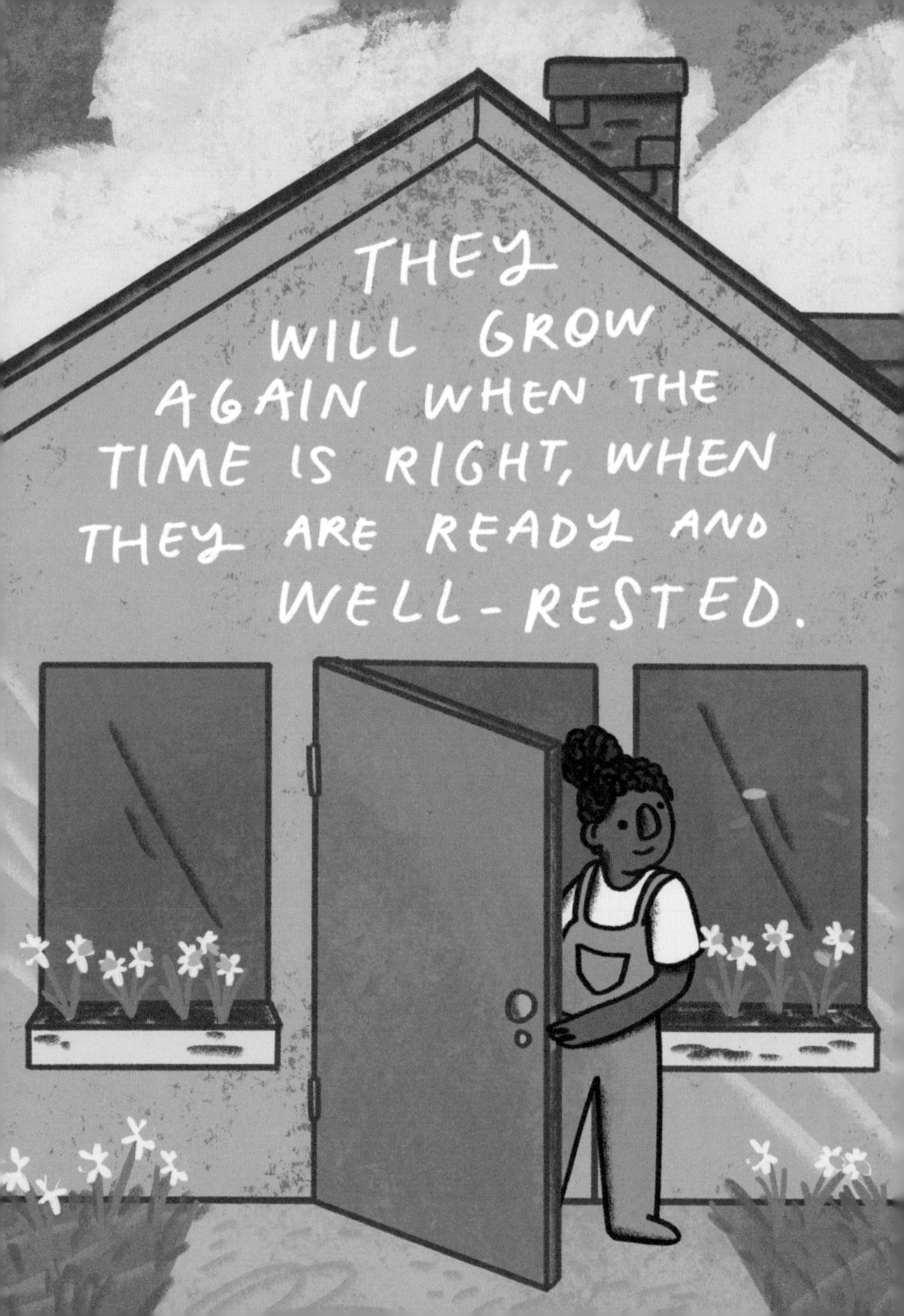
THEY WILL GROW AGAIN WHEN THE TIME IS RIGHT, WHEN THEY ARE READY AND WELL-RESTED.

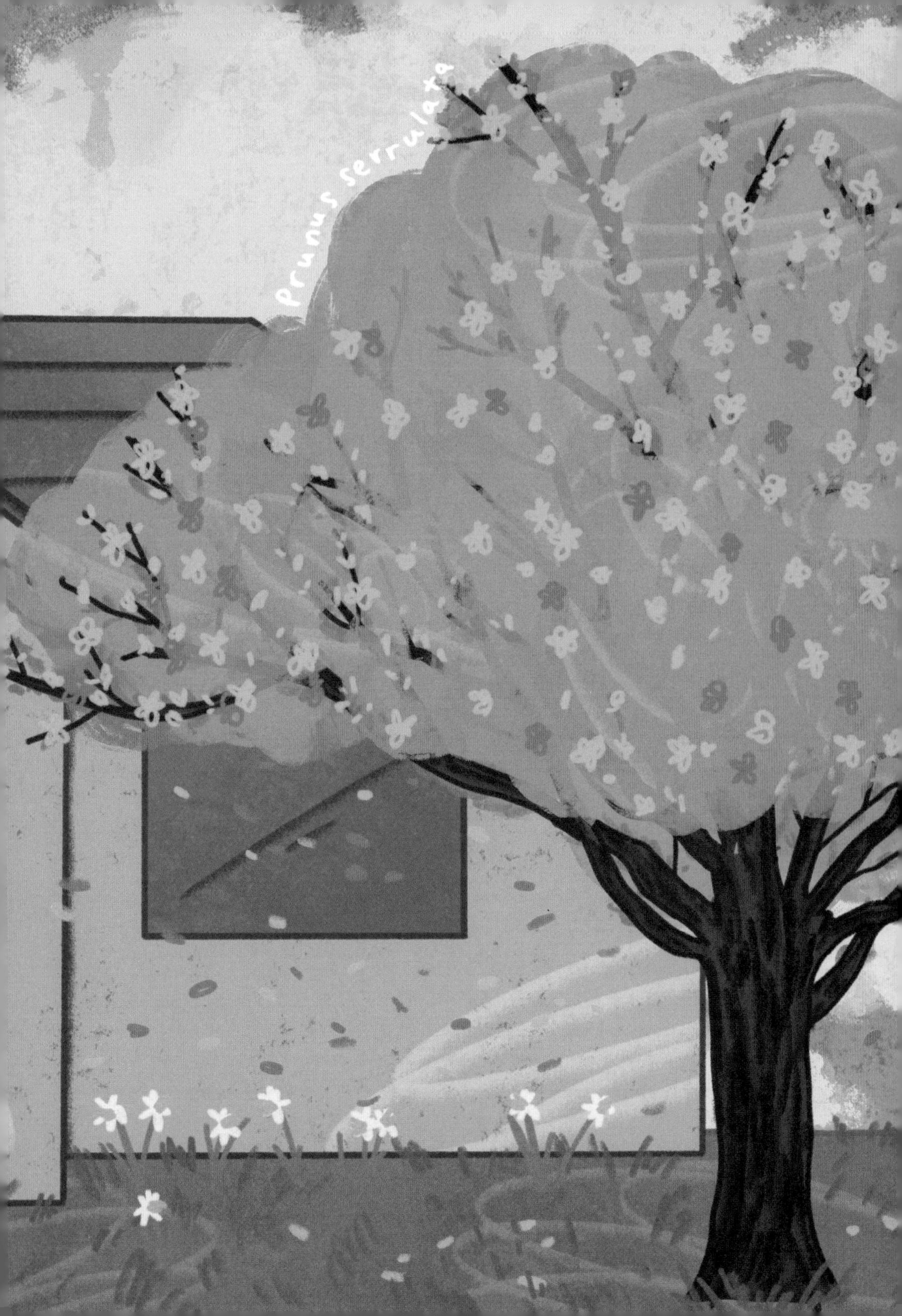
Prunus serrulata

HOW TO GO DORMANT, AND THEN COME BACK

STEP 1
PLAN AHEAD

REST WORKS BEST WHEN WE CAN ANTICIPATE ITS ARRIVAL.

If you know when it's coming, like the annual approach of winter or your days off at the end of a workweek, you can begin to plan accordingly.

MON.	TUES.	WEDS.	THURS.	FRI.
WORK	WORK	MORE WORK	ALSO WORK	REST!!

MON.	TUES.	WEDS.	THURS.	FRI.
WORK AGAIN	UGH STILL WORK	OK I GOT THIS?	ONE MORE DAY!	REST!!

MON.	TUES.	WEDS.	THURS.	FRI.
OK BACK TO IT.	WORK!	HALFWAY THERE!	I FEEL.... GOOD!?!	REST!!

WHAT IS YOUR WINTER?

When are you at your weakest? How can you accommodate that time by going dormant? Scarce times don't always come on schedule and they don't look the same for everyone.

Virginia bluebells, for example, burst into bloom each spring and go dormant in the summer when the temperature gets too hot.

Mertensia virginica

If you can become aware of when your own nourishment will be at its weakest, you can effectively plan to rest when it will benefit you the most—and sustain you well into the future.

THINKING AHEAD, WRAP UP THAT STAGE OF THE PROJECT OR TRY TO REACH A COMFORTABLE PLACE TO PAUSE BEFORE GOING DORMANT.

In colder climates, the tubers of tender plants like begonias are dug up and kept in a cool, dry, dark place to pass the winter indoors.

KNOWING THAT YOUR REST IS COMING WILL MAKE THE NEXT PART EASIER.

STEP 2
HONOR YOUR DORMANCY

DO NOT OPEN UNTIL WELL-RESTED!

It is instilled in us from an early age that to "succeed" (whatever that means), we must constantly be producing, constantly be working.

TIME, WE'RE TAUGHT, IS A THING TO BE WASTED OR SPENT.

BUT IS A TREE WASTING TIME WHEN IT DROPS ITS LEAVES IN AUTUMN? OR DOES IT KNOW SOMETHING THAT WE SIMPLY HAVEN'T LEARNED YET?

THERE ARE MANY WAYS TO SHED YOUR LEAVES:

LIE IN BED READING A NOVEL. ALL DAY.

HAND WRITE A LETTER TO SOMEONE YOU LOVE AND MAIL IT TO THEM.

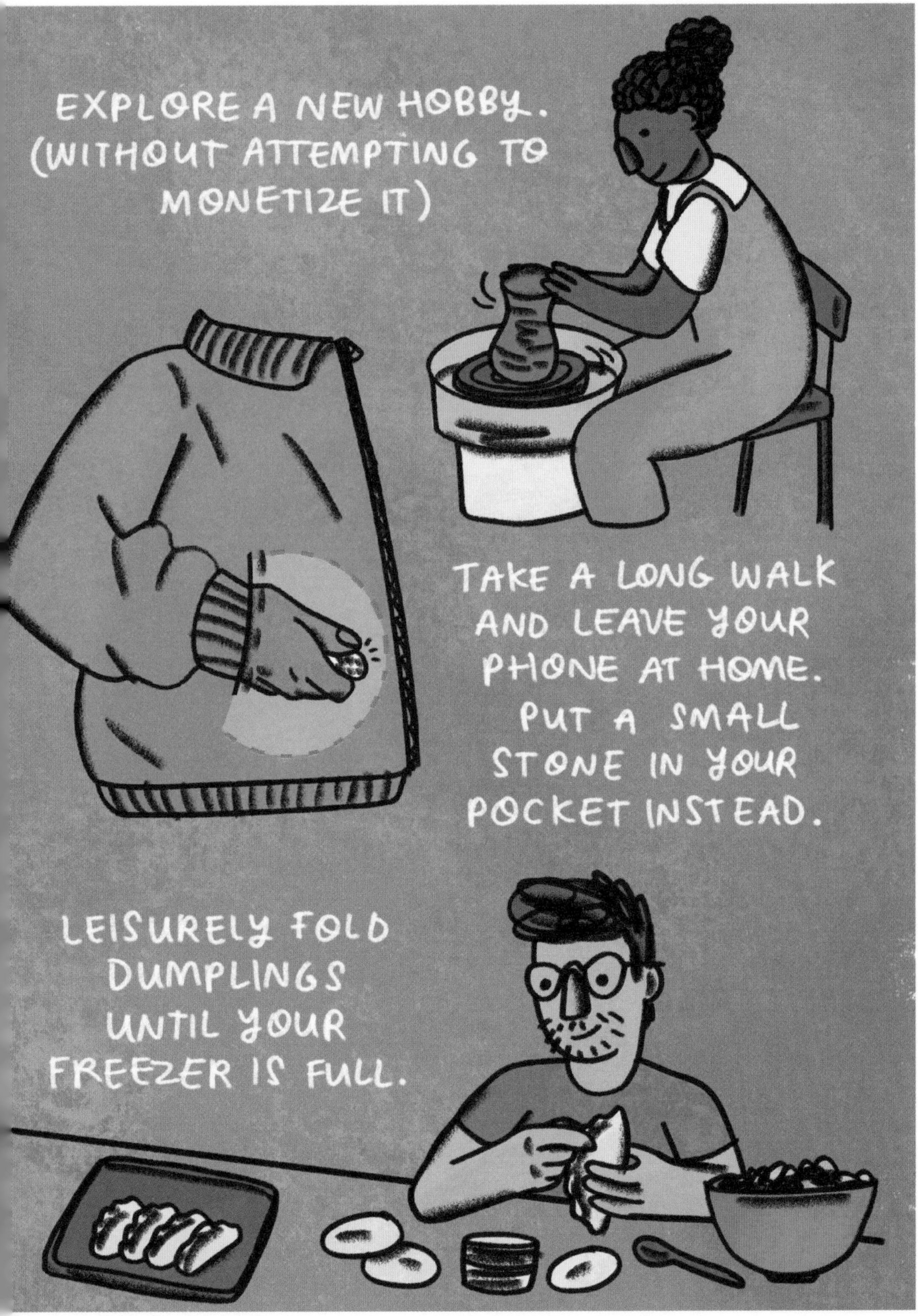
EXPLORE A NEW HOBBY.
(WITHOUT ATTEMPTING TO
MONETIZE IT)
TAKE A LONG WALK
AND LEAVE YOUR
PHONE AT HOME.
PUT A SMALL
STONE IN YOUR
POCKET INSTEAD.
LEISURELY FOLD
DUMPLINGS
UNTIL YOUR
FREEZER IS FULL.

RESPECT YOUR REST

It's tempting to think that we could forgo the need for rest if only the circumstances were right. If our resources are never scarce, if we're excited about our careers, have loved ones who support us, and hobbies that engage us—then why bother going dormant? But for many plants, this "eternal summer" can actually be a great detriment.

Certain deciduous trees, like the Japanese maple, when provided with warmth and sunlight year-round, will force themselves into dormancy after a few years. They've been working constantly and they're in desperate need of a break. You could say they're experiencing burnout. And once they've gone dormant, they require a sustained period of cold (but not freezing) temperatures to wake up from their rest, a signal that the worst has passed and it's time to get back to work. This process is called vernalization, and if it's too warm, the maples will stay dormant and eventually die.

Their dormant phase is a necessary resting point, but it's also a critical means with which they regulate their growth. Anticipating when to rest helps them to know how long to rest—and when to grow. The two are inextricably linked and equally essential.

REST IS VITAL.

Your very life depends on it. Friendships, family, your work, your home—they will all benefit from the occasional dormant phase.

Rest not only ensures that what you're doing is the best it can be, but that it can remain that way far into the future.

WITHOUT GOING DORMANT IN THE WINTER, THERE ARE NO FLOWERS IN THE SPRING.

LOOK FOR SIGNS THAT IT'S TIME TO WAKE UP AGAIN

Even if you know your period of rest is coming
to an end, it can be tricky to jump back
in. The inertia that must be overcome to
get back to work can be tremendous.

YOU MAY EVEN BE AFRAID.

What if I can't make
them bloom again?

What if I can't
remember how?

What if they're dead?

GULP

It requires a good bit of courage to spring back into action—but it's nothing to be afraid of.

JUST TAKE IT SLOW.

Ease yourself back in. Take lots of breaks along the way. It's totally normal to feel a bit rusty at first.

Remember: Waking up from a dormant spell is a big job. It doesn't happen all at once.

Pay attention to your feelings. Keep an eye out for the sun and the changes in the weather. Eventually, you will see that it is time to work again.

SOMETHING WILL TELL YOU THAT THE TIME IS RIGHT.

Begonia x tuberosa

TRUST THAT FEELING.

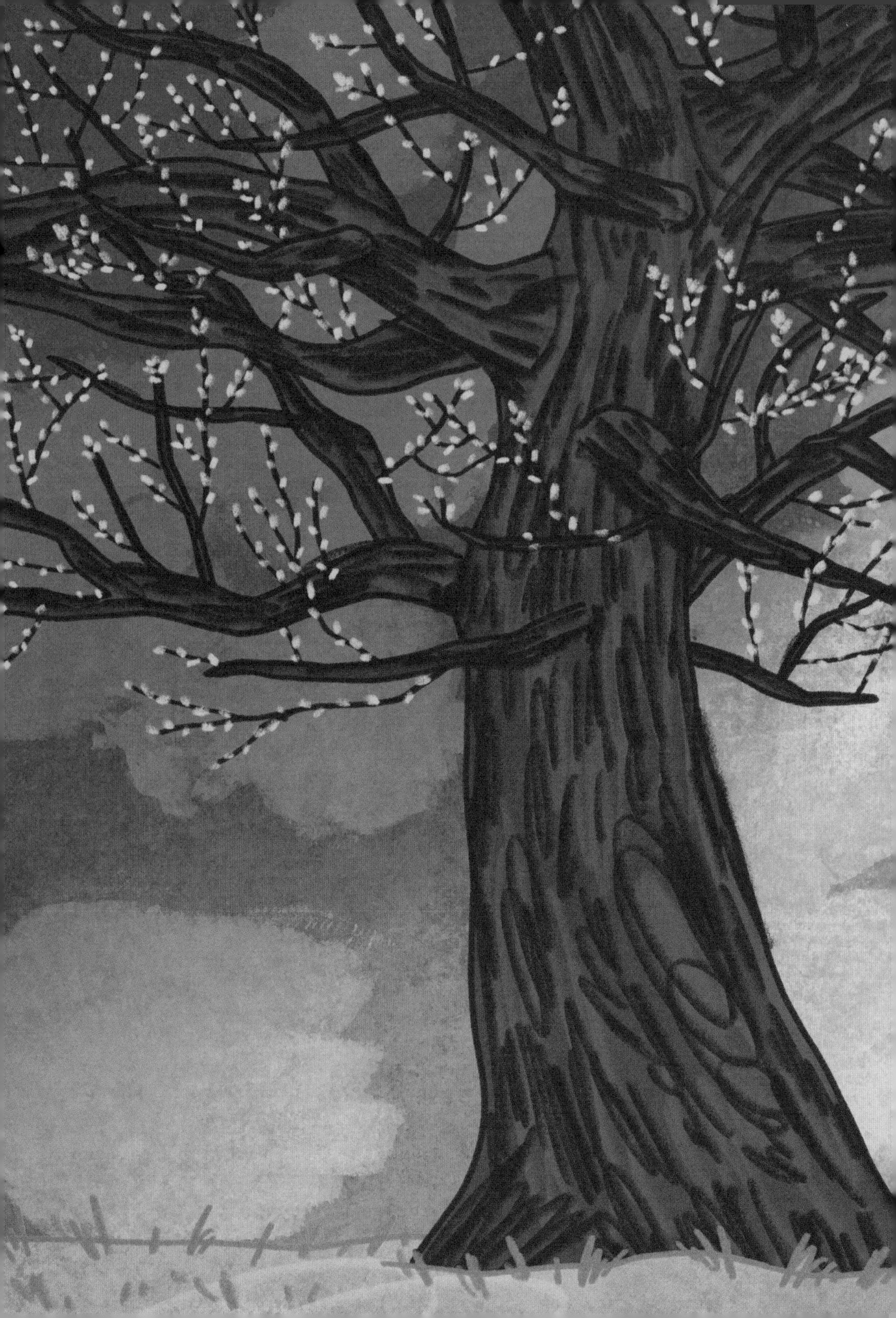

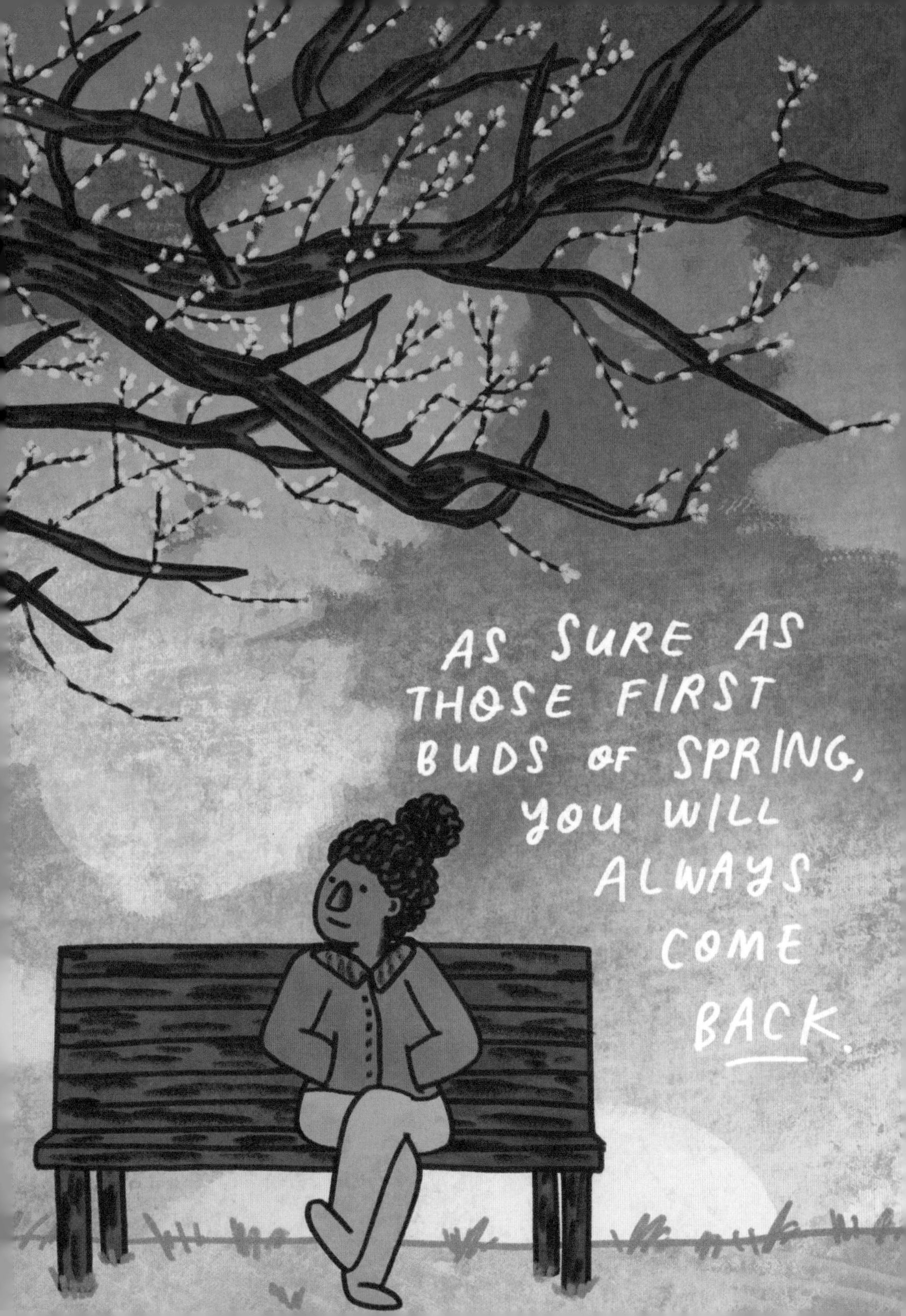
AS SURE AS THOSE FIRST BUDS OF SPRING, YOU WILL ALWAYS COME BACK.

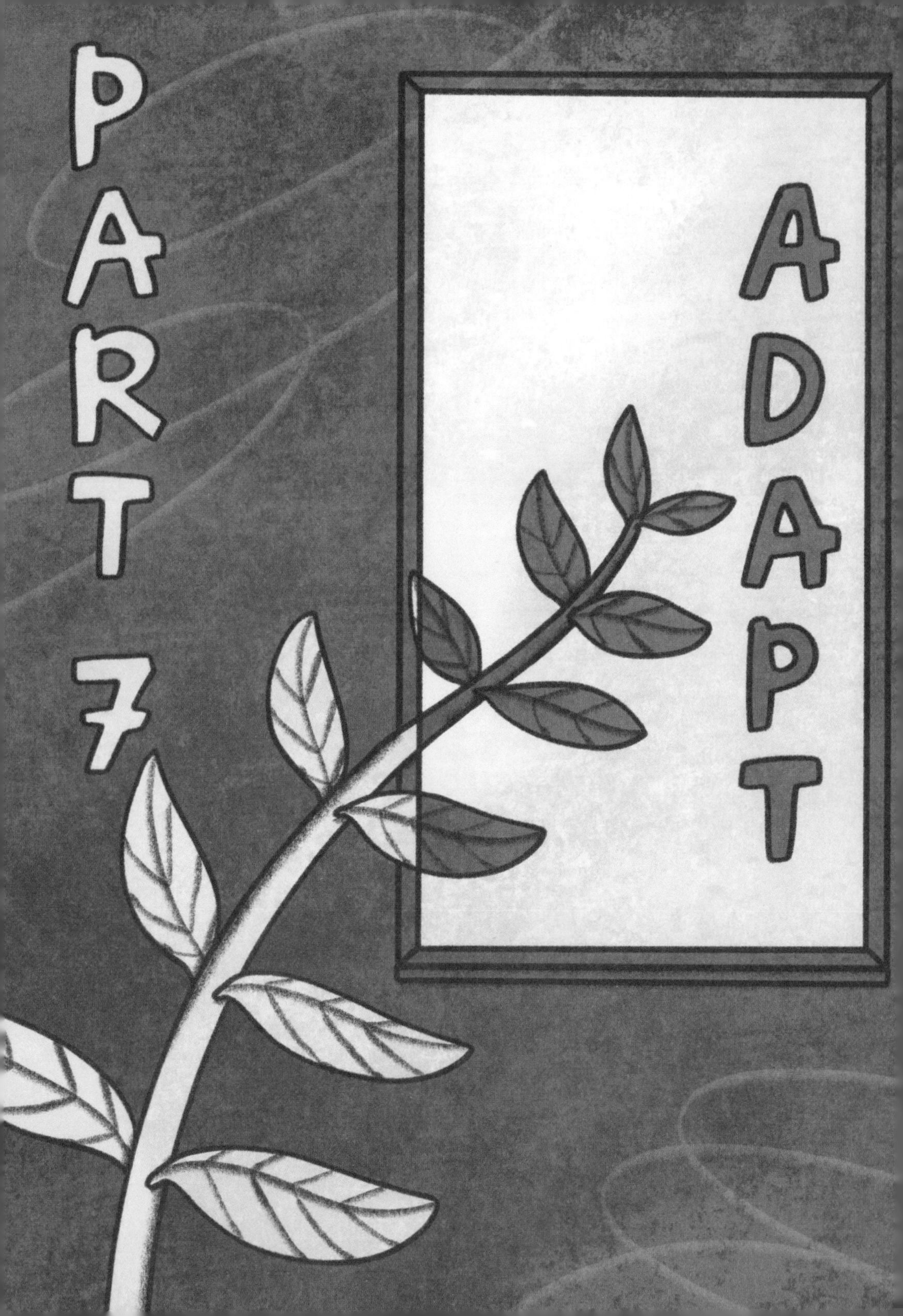
PART 7
ADAPT

PLANTS ARE EXCELLENT AT
GETTING WHAT THEY NEED.

BECAUSE THEY CAN'T JUST GET UP AND LEAVE WHEN THINGS GET HARD, THEY ARE ADEPT AT THE ART OF ADAPTING.

Campsis radicans

MANY UNPLEASANT THINGS CAN HAPPEN TO A PLANT:

Roots can rot in soil that is too moist.

Fungus can take hold in foliage that has grown too dense.

Bugs can devour a crop of vegetables within days.

Too much sun or heat can scorch delicate leaves.

THESE TYPES OF CHALLENGES CAN BE PREVENTED.

We can tend to the soil, we can cut away infected foliage, and we can take advantage of companion planting and horticultural oils to keep would-be pests at bay.

Cucumis sativus

For most problems like these, there is a helpful tool kit we can reach for.

BUT WHAT ABOUT THE CHALLENGES WE CAN'T PREVENT?

What about the situations when the very *environment* is at odds with your growth?

When the soil is too dry or there just isn't enough light?

When your job is exhausting but you've got bills to pay . . .

. . . or when you've moved back in with your parents to save some money but GOSH you're ready to get your own place again.

Asplenium nidus

IF YOU CANNOT MOVE, YOU MUST ADAPT.

ADAPTATION IS EVERYWHERE

IN THE PLANT WORLD.

It's mangroves sitting atop stiltlike aquatic roots that can filter out salt from brackish water.

It's wildflowers growing through the cracks in the sidewalk.

It's the gnarled, thousand-year-old trees precariously clinging to the sides of cliffs.

It's philodendrons on forest floors with leaves large enough to catch what little sunlight filters through the canopy.

It's cacti blooming at night so their delicate blossoms don't shrivel in the desert heat.

ADAPTATION IS THE FUEL FOR DIVERSITY.

FAMILY: ASTERACEAE

CHAMOMILE

CHICORY

OXEYE DAISY

MARIGOLD

CONEFLOWER

DANDELION

CORNFLOWER

LETTUCE

ZINNIA

MILK THISTLE

GOLDENROD

COSMO

YARROW

SUNFLOWER

PURPLE ASTER

ARTICHOKE

It is the primary reason plants are as unique and abundant as they are. The taxonomic family *Asteraceae*, for example, has more than twenty-four thousand unique species, many of them familiar to us. Adaptation may be a challenge, but that resilience is something to celebrate.

HOW TO ADAPT WHEN IT FEELS LIKE THE WORLD IS AGAINST YOU

STEP 1
BE HONEST

Ask yourself—are you in an adapt situation or a *get out* situation? Unlike plants, we can usually get up and go when things are really, truly terrible.

IF YOUR GUT IS TELLING YOU TO GET OUT, THEN GET OUT!

STEP 2
COMMIT

If you're going to stay, *decide* to stay. After all, you planted your seed here for a reason: There has to be something worth sticking around for. It may not be easy, but try to accept—for the time being at least—that you cannot change your circumstances.

BY COMMITTING TO YOUR INTENTION TO STAY, YOU ARE MAKING A COMMITMENT TO ADAPTING.

TRY TO
REMEMBER WHY
YOU CHOSE THIS PLACE.

Was it different then,
and something
changed?

Or maybe you hoped something
would change—and it didn't?

CONSIDER WHY YOU ARE STAYING.

Is it for independence or family
or the bright, sunny weather?

What does
future you
look like?

Will this place
help you get
there?

IT IS MUCH EASIER TO ADAPT WHEN YOU KNOW YOUR PURPOSE FOR DOING SO.

peperomia
tetraphylla

STEP 3
IDENTIFY WHAT YOU'RE MISSING

To effectively adapt, you've got to know what it is you're lacking.

Is your soil too dry or the sunlight too sparse?

Are you missing companionship? Money? Privacy? A critical tool?

Figure out what specifically you're missing and you might just be able to come up with a short-term solution—and gain some insight into how long you'll have to wait it out.

ACKNOWLEDGING THAT YOUR CIRCUMSTANCES WILL NOT BE FOREVER CAN MAKE IT MUCH EASIER TO WITHSTAND THEM.

GET CREATIVE

Adaptation doesn't happen overnight, and it rarely arrives with an obvious solution. A lot of things we do to adapt are things we never would have thought to do otherwise.

Monotropa uniflora.

"Ghost pipes" are plants that grow on dense forest floors. They have adapted to the dark by acquiring their nutrients from fungi in the soil; they do not photosynthesize. Since they have no green chlorophyll, they are typically white or pink.

IN A WEIRD WAY, ADAPTATION CAN ACTUALLY HELP YOU BE MORE CREATIVE.

IT'S OKAY TO TAKE YOUR TIME

Even in a healthy, diverse forest, it can be tough for a tree to grow. The largest, oldest trees form a dense canopy, shadowing the forest floor and making it nearly impossible for any new growth to break through. Billions of seeds hit the ground every year, and only a select few ever make it more than a foot high. But some trees, like European beeches, play the long game. A beech tree half your height and no thicker than your index finger could very well be more than eighty years old. They have been adapting from the moment they sprouted, slowing their growth to a near halt; they are biding their time.

Because eventually, an opportunity will arise. A mature tree—hundreds of years old—will die, and the sky will open up. The tree will become brittle with time, and may fall or split and come crashing down to the ground, leaving a clearing of sunlight in its wake. Now everything changes: The "young" trees adjust their metabolism. They start growing much more rapidly, racing their way to the top, getting as high as they can before the clearing fills in with new branches from the towering giants. It may be a few more decades before another clearing opens up and the younger trees can join them up in the canopy.

But for now, they're halfway there—and they've glimpsed what great heights await them.

It may not be glamorous, and it may not be everything you had hoped for, but eventually change will come.

Fagus sylvatica

You will grow beyond your hardships, and the things that once constrained you will soon feel small and distant.

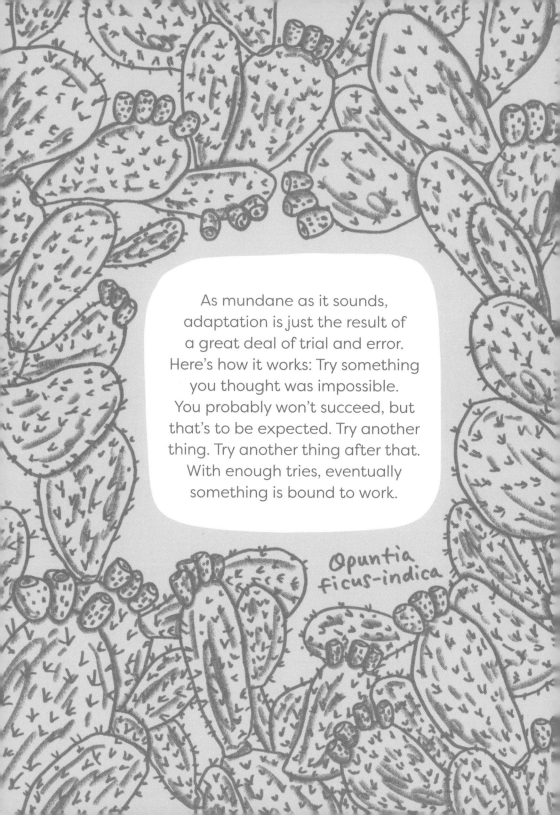

As mundane as it sounds, adaptation is just the result of a great deal of trial and error. Here's how it works: Try something you thought was impossible. You probably won't succeed, but that's to be expected. Try another thing. Try another thing after that. With enough tries, eventually something is bound to work.

Opuntia ficus-indica

ENDURE

NOTHING LASTS FOREVER—AND IN SOME CASES, THAT CAN BE A GOOD THING.

Conditions change. Ecosystems ebb and flow. Given enough time, mountains can rise up out of the oceans, and deserts can give way to lush tropical rainforests.

Nitraria retusa

Around eight thousand years ago, the Sahara Desert transformed into a rainforest. Thousands of years later, it became a desert again. How long until its next transformation?

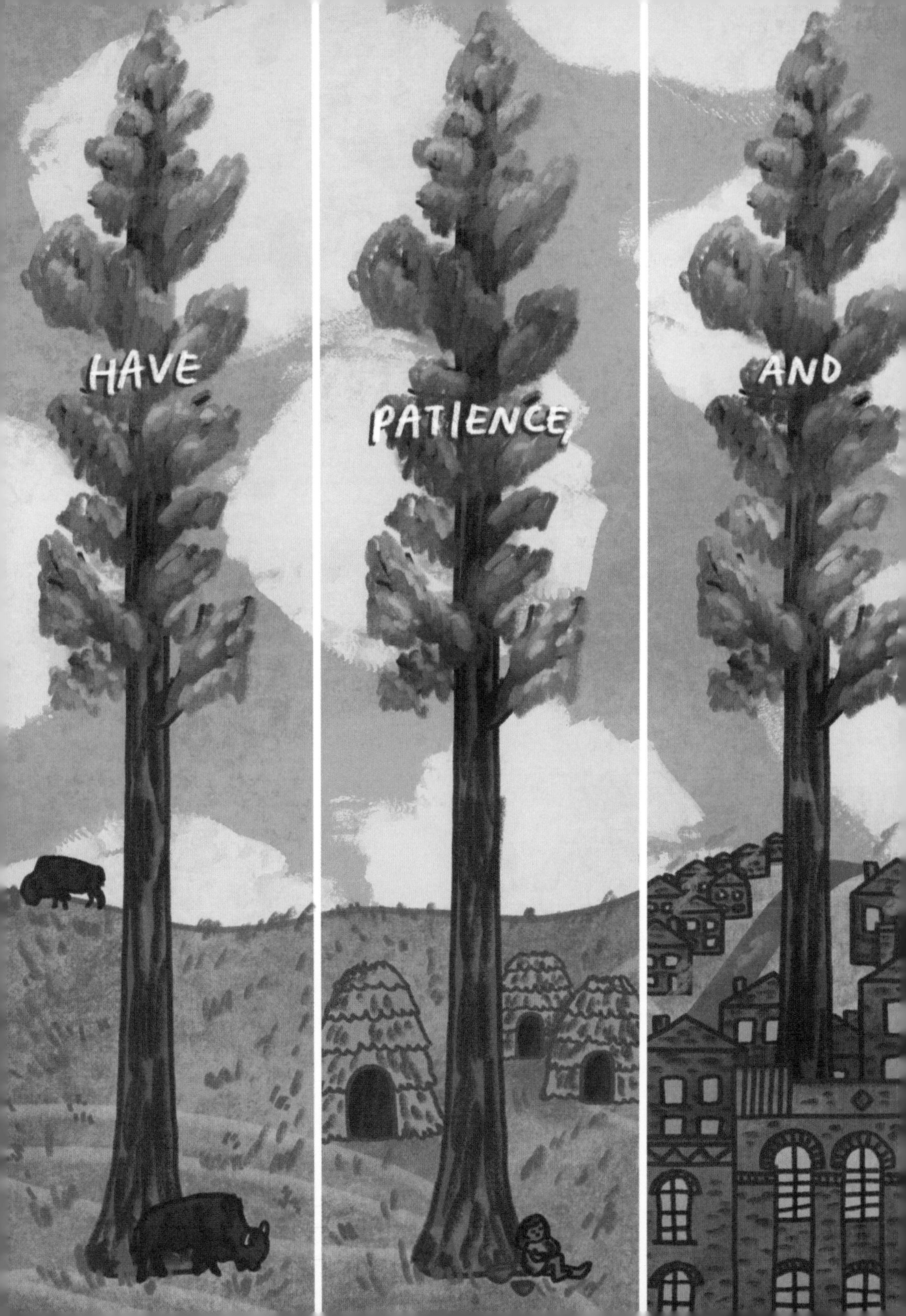
HAVE
PATIENCE,
AND

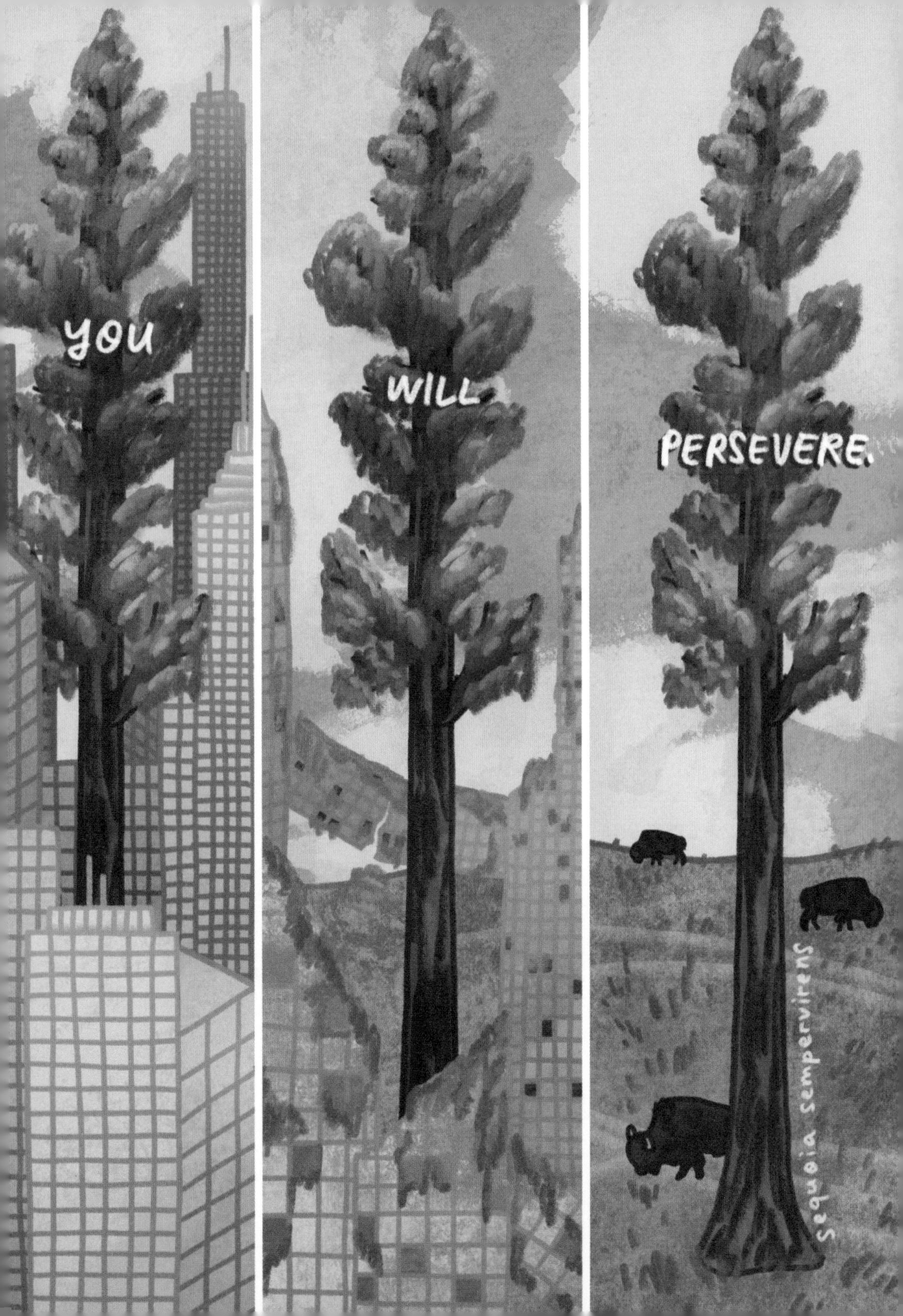
YOU
WILL
PERSEVERE.
Sequoia sempervirens

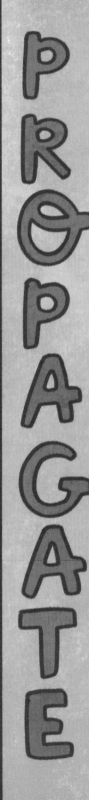

PART 8

PROPAGATE

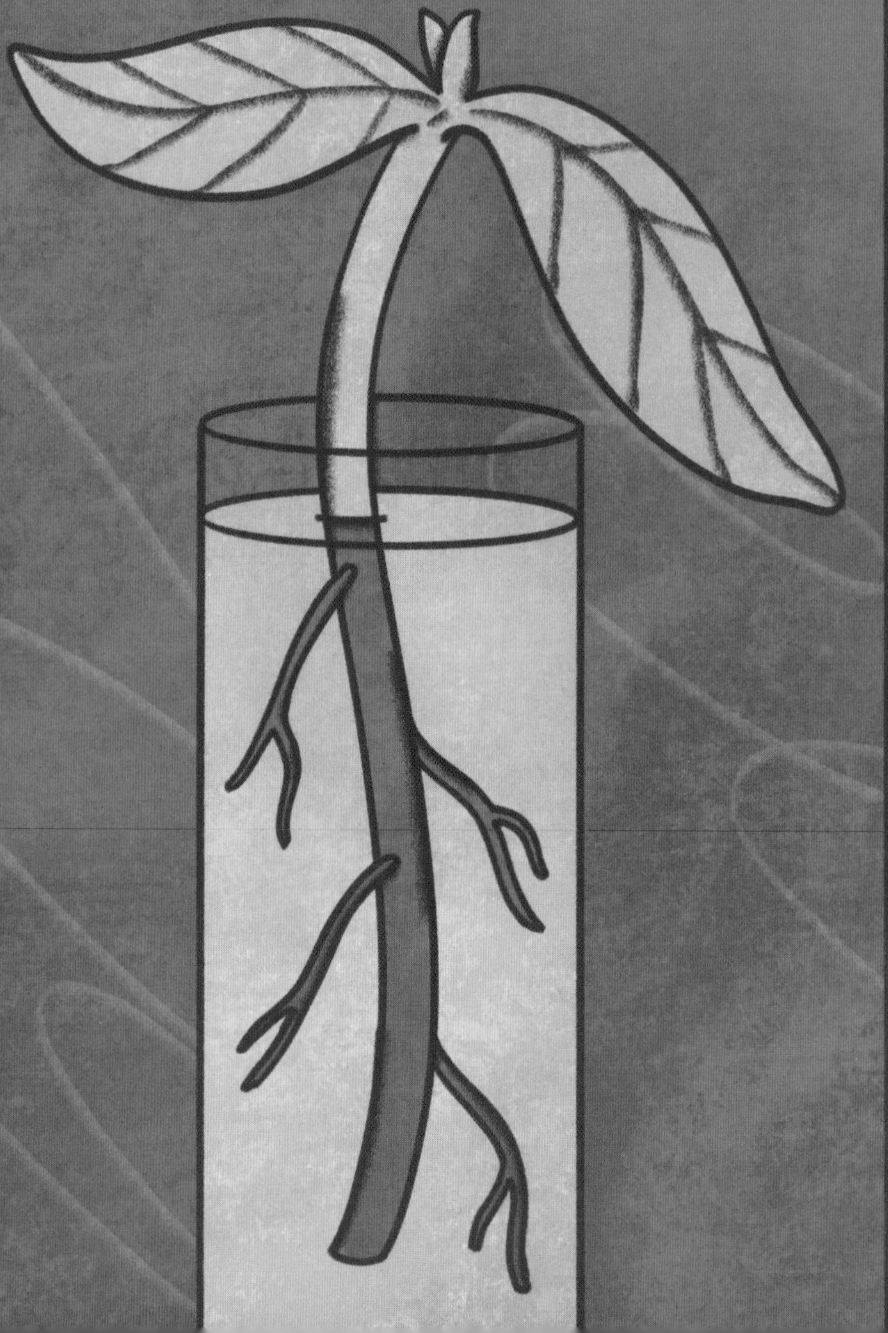

WHILE MANY PLANTS APPEAR TO SIMPLY GROW ENDLESSLY,

Hedera helix

THAT ISN'T USUALLY THEIR ULTIMATE GOAL.

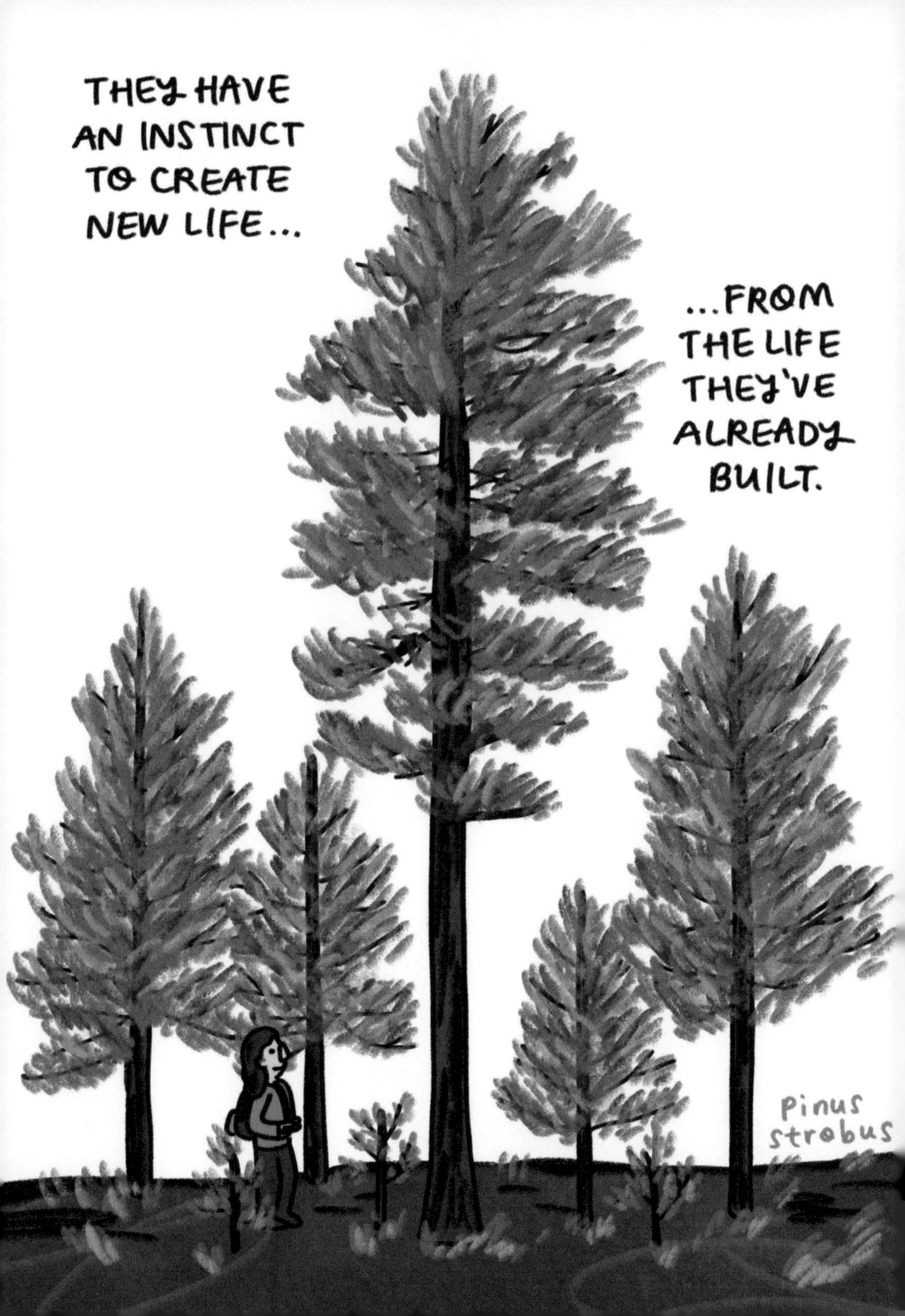
THEY HAVE AN INSTINCT TO CREATE NEW LIFE...
...FROM THE LIFE THEY'VE ALREADY BUILT.
Pinus strobus

EVEN THE TALLEST, OLDEST TREE ON EARTH CAN ONLY GROW SO FAR ON ITS OWN.

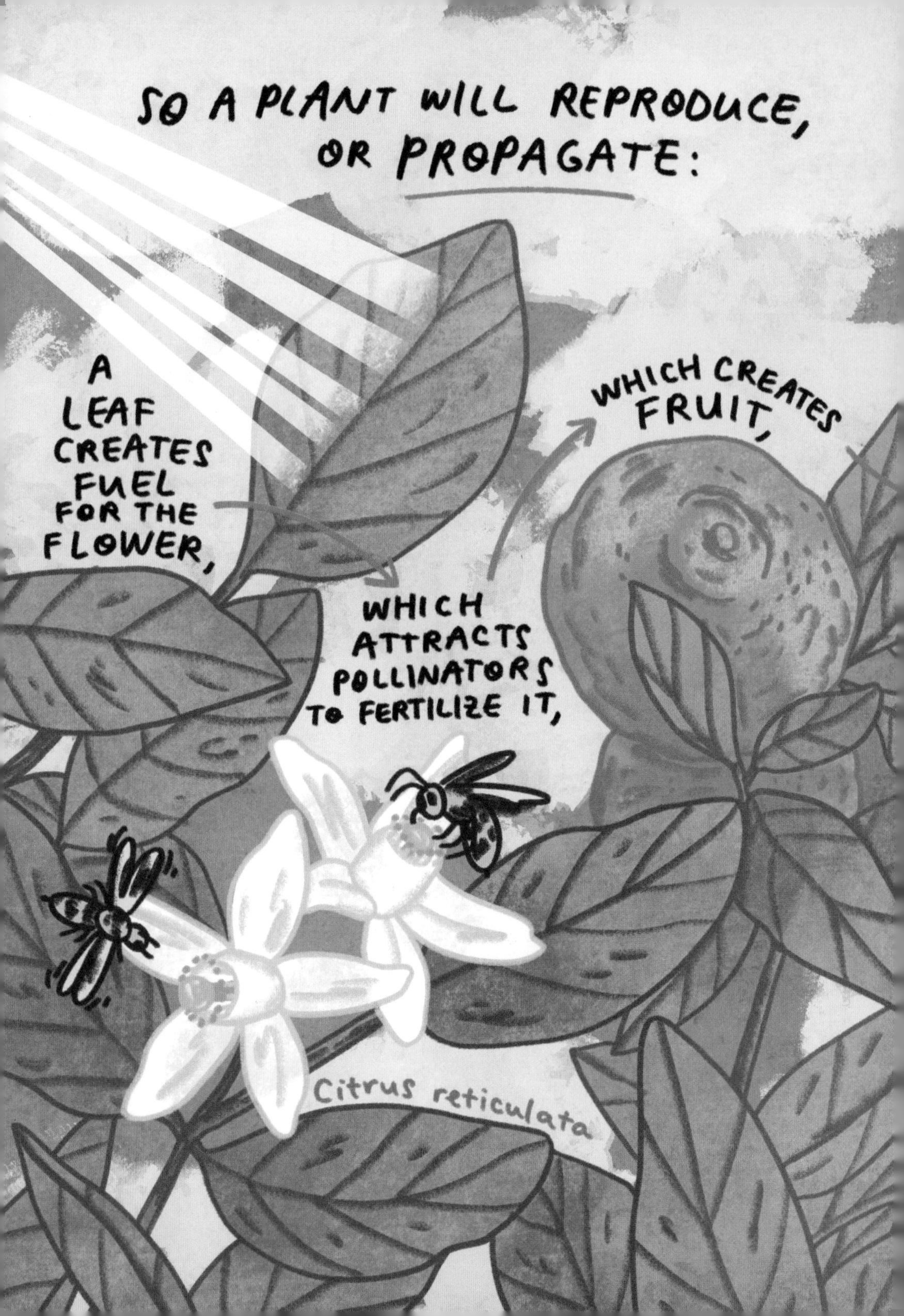
SO A PLANT WILL REPRODUCE, OR PROPAGATE:
A LEAF CREATES FUEL FOR THE FLOWER,
WHICH ATTRACTS POLLINATORS TO FERTILIZE IT,
WHICH CREATES FRUIT,
Citrus reticulata

WHICH CREATES SEEDS,

SO THAT A *NEW* VERSION OF THE PLANT CAN GROW —

AND SO ON,

Remember that seed you found? Long before you ever stumbled upon it, long before you planted it and tended to it and turned it into what it is today, it was propagated by some distant flower, tucked inside a fruit, hanging from a tree: a tiny possibility, waiting for someone like you to come along and help it grow.

FOREVER.

By creating multiple versions of itself, a plant ensures that no matter what bad things may happen to one of them, there are always others still alive.

ITS LEGACY CONTINUES IN WHATEVER NEW FORM IT TAKES.

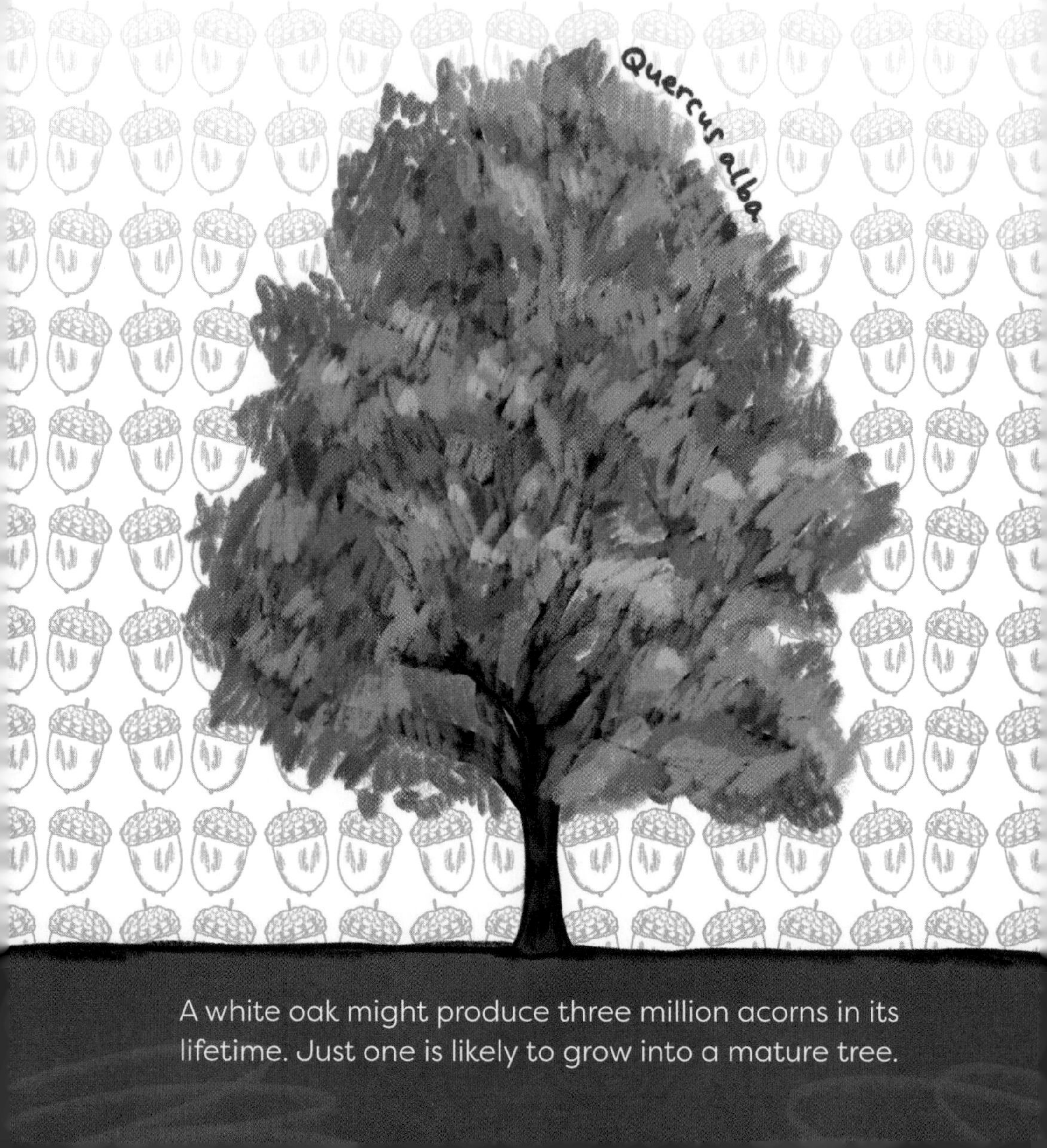
Quercus alba

A white oak might produce three million acorns in its lifetime. Just one is likely to grow into a mature tree.

And it's not always through a seed that
a plant may replicate itself.

THERE ARE MANY WAYS TO BRING NEW LIFE INTO THE WORLD.

Chinese money plants can propagate from rhizomes—horizontal stems that spread underground—sending up new shoots as they go.

Spider plants can propagate with aerial stems called stolons, which branch away from the plant, producing new roots and leaves from those stems.

These new shoots can simply be cut away and repotted to grow into a new generation. Many plants, if cut cleanly and in the right place, will sprout new roots just sitting in a glass of water on a sunny windowsill.

A PLANT THAT IS PROPAGATED FROM A CUTTING WILL GROW STRONG AND MATURE MUCH MORE QUICKLY THAN ONE GROWN FROM A SEED. IT TAKES INTO ACCOUNT EVERYTHING YOU'VE LEARNED SO FAR.

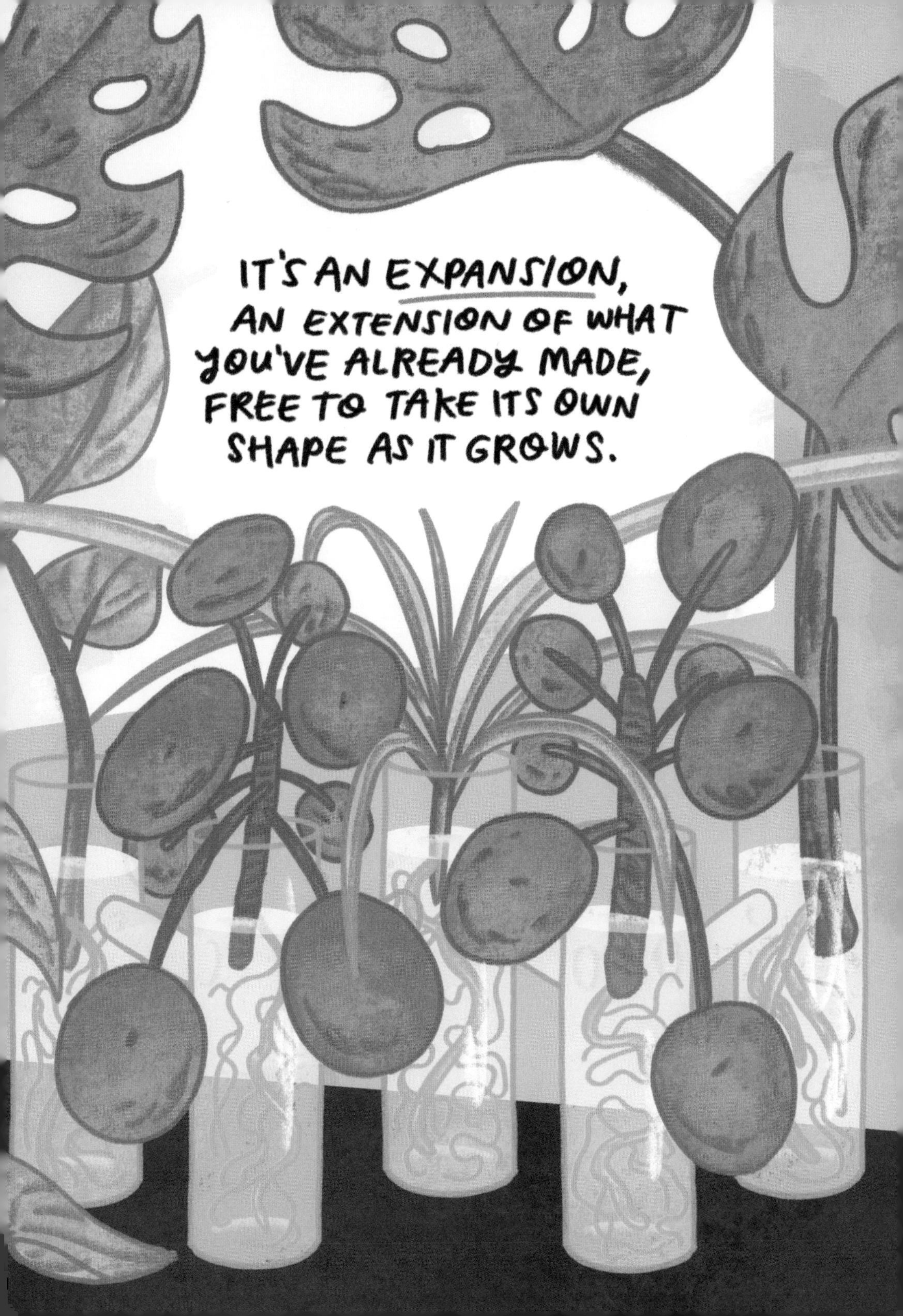
IT'S AN EXPANSION, AN EXTENSION OF WHAT YOU'VE ALREADY MADE, FREE TO TAKE ITS OWN SHAPE AS IT GROWS.

HOW TO TURN ONE PLANT INTO MANY

STEP 1
LET IT REACH MATURITY

No, this has nothing to do with age.

A plant will not propagate well until it has matured. But "maturity" here is not about the amount of time that has passed. Don't confuse it with being *wise* or *perfect* or *complete*.

THERE IS NO END HERE, ONLY GROWTH.

When the plant you are tending to has been growing steadily for a while, safely and with reliable nourishment, it may be safe to say it has matured.

Rosa chinensis

Only you will know how long that "while" is and when it has grown enough to take on the next challenge.

STEP 2
SET A PIECE ASIDE

WHEN YOUR PLANT IS FLOURISHING, IT'S A GOOD TIME TO TAKE A CUTTING — TO CREATE SOMETHING NEW FROM THE WORK YOU'VE ALREADY DONE.

Now that you've reached a comfortable point in your growth, how can you branch out?

How can you take what you've learned so far and apply it to something new?

TAKE AS MANY CUTTINGS AS YOU CAN COMFORTABLY CARE FOR. PUT THEM ALL IN WATER IN A SUNNY SPOT WHERE THEY WILL BE ABLE TO THRIVE.

TEND TO THE CUTTINGS

Like a seedling, cuttings can still be quite fragile in these early days. Change their water periodically. Clip off any parts that die. Check in on them often.

Within just a few weeks, your cuttings will begin to sprout roots and unfurl new leaves.

peperomia orba

The parent plant lives on, too, but requires less maintenance now.

It is not unlike growing a plant from seed, but this new one you didn't have to search for.

IT HAS ALREADY BEEN GROWING THIS ENTIRE TIME.

KEEP SOME FOR YOURSELF

It's good to have a few things going at once—
several cuttings, a stack of library books, a
handful of blossoming friendships—

some things to tend to when you get bored
or tired or just want to mix things up a bit.

These new endeavors will soon grow to maturity, too. Your original plant is multiplying and each of its offspring will bear their own with time.

YOU ARE SETTING YOURSELF UP FOR A LIFETIME OF ABUNDANCE.

And it all started with just one seed.

GIVE THE REST AWAY

OUR OWN FLOURISHING ALSO HELPS OTHERS TO FLOURISH, THE MORE WE ARE WILLING TO SHARE. GIVING AWAY AN ESTABLISHED CUTTING IS A WAY TO TAKE WHAT YOU HAVE ACCOMPLISHED SO FAR AND PASS IT DOWN THE LINE.

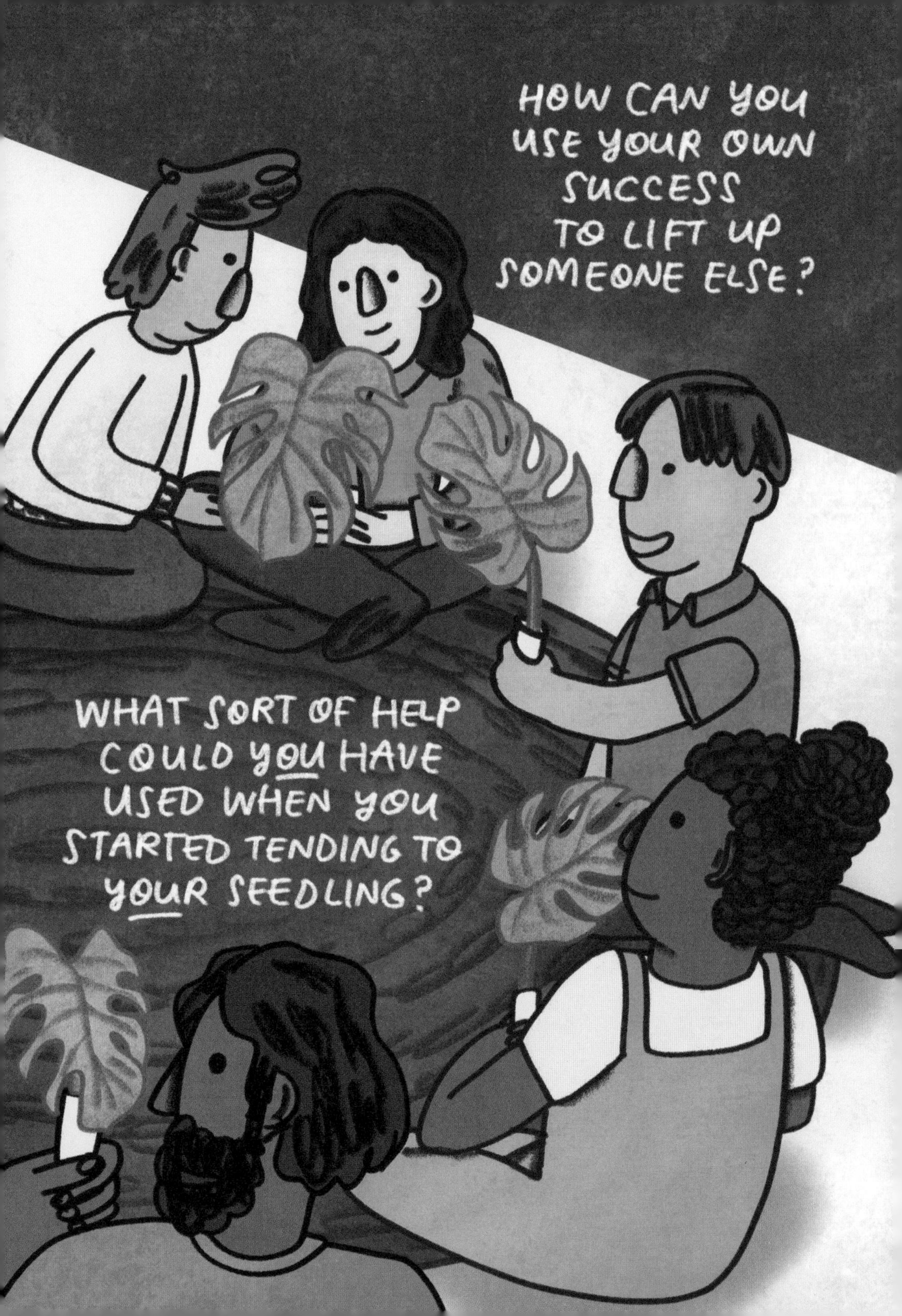
HOW CAN YOU USE YOUR OWN SUCCESS TO LIFT UP SOMEONE ELSE?
WHAT SORT OF HELP COULD YOU HAVE USED WHEN YOU STARTED TENDING TO YOUR SEEDLING?

THERE'S A REASON PROPAGATION REQUIRES MATURITY.

You must be comfortable enough with the merit of your own growth that you can use your energy to uplift others without feeling threatened.

Acknowledge that your own flourishing was in some part due to someone who came before you—and now you can be that person for someone else.

IMAGINE THE ABUNDANCE AND DIVERSITY OF A WILD MEADOW.

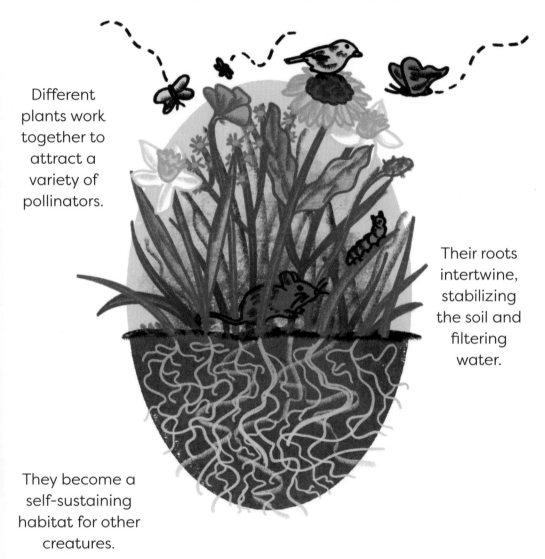

Different plants work together to attract a variety of pollinators.

Their roots intertwine, stabilizing the soil and filtering water.

They become a self-sustaining habitat for other creatures.

TOGETHER THEY ALLOW LIFE TO CONTINUE, EVER EXPANDING, EVER EVOLVING.

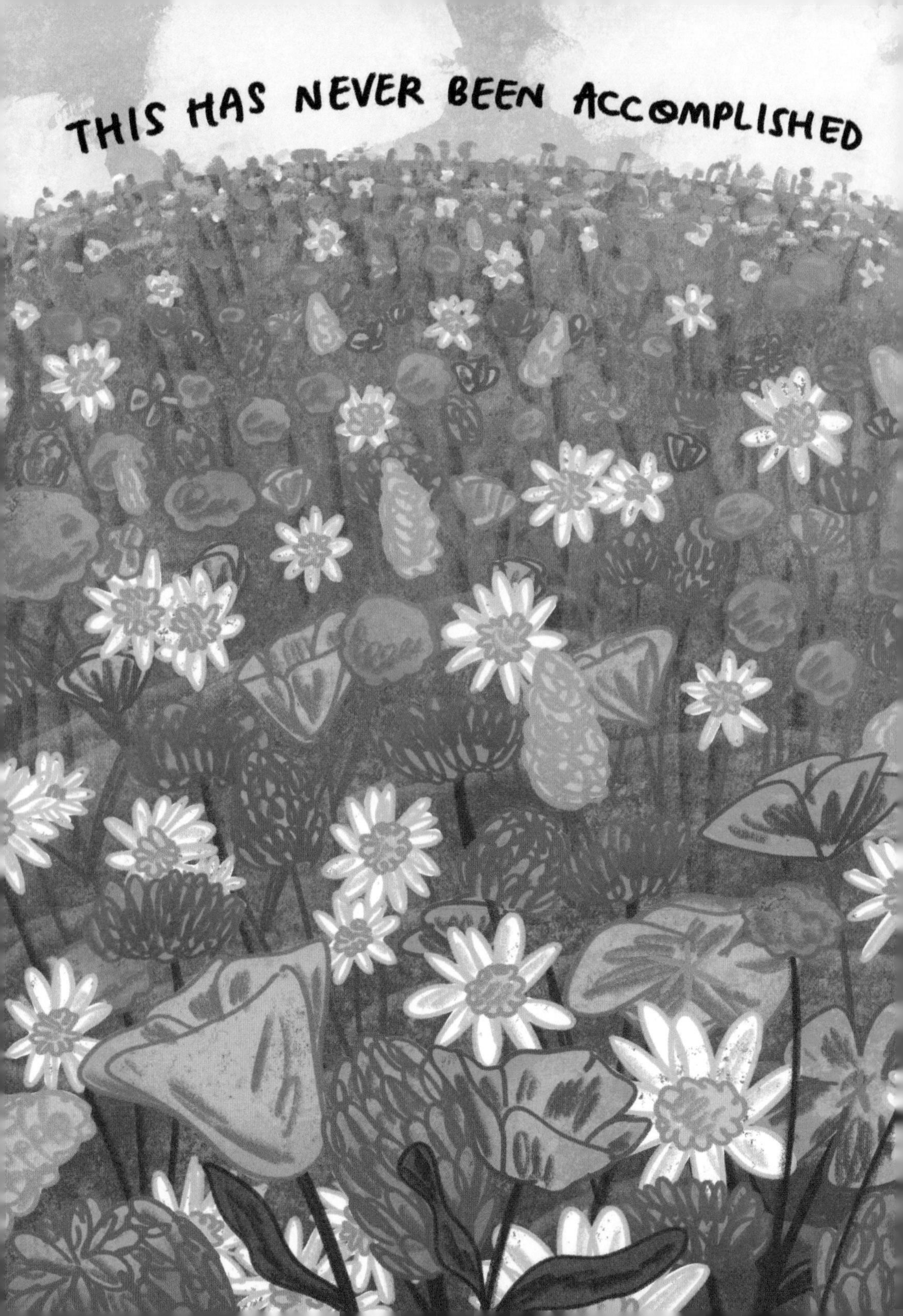
THIS HAS NEVER BEEN ACCOMPLISHED

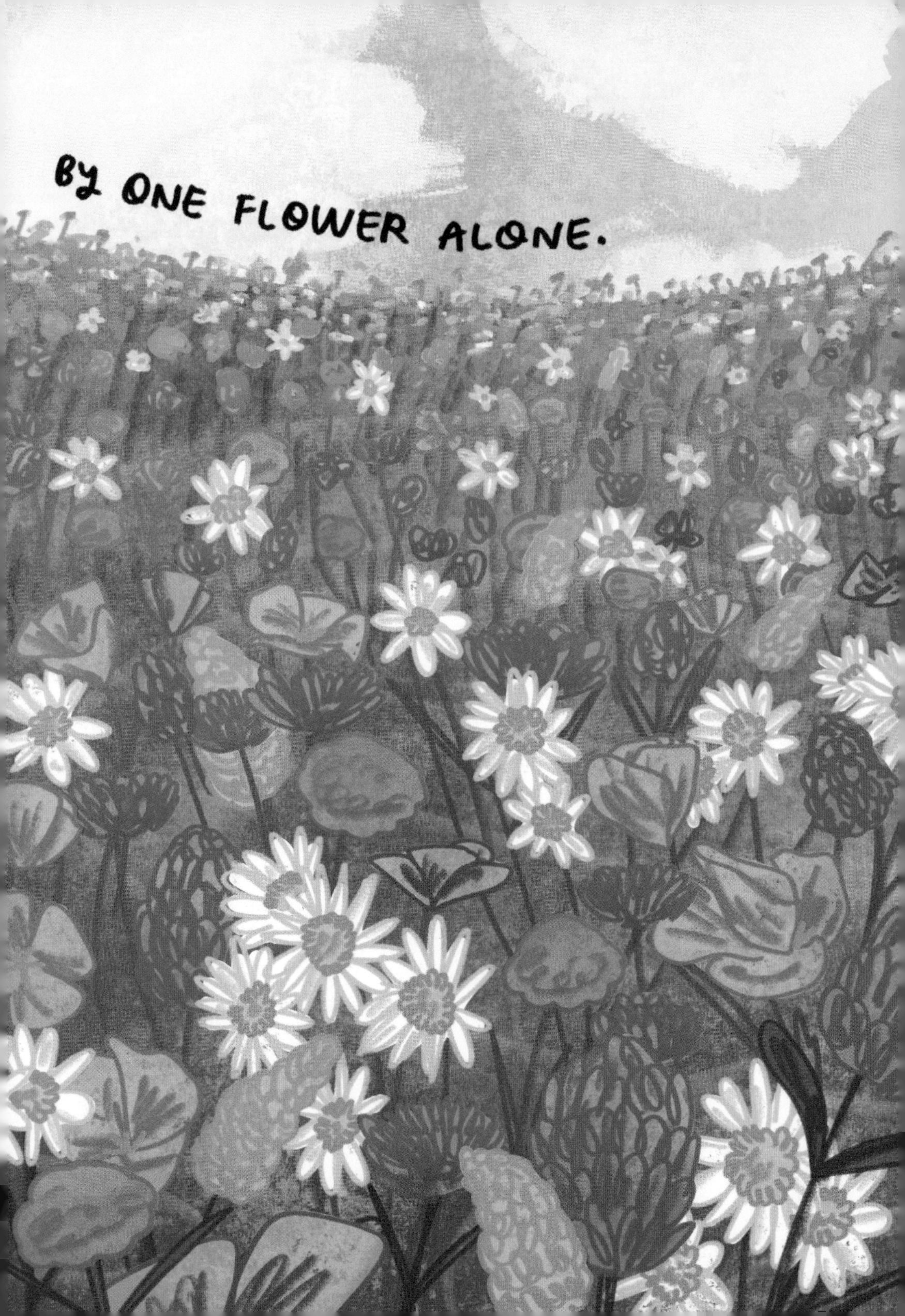
BY ONE FLOWER ALONE.

PART 9
PRUNE

THERE ARE MANY REASONS WHY
A PLANT MAY BE IN NEED OF PRUNING.

MOST PLANTS ARE RESILIENT AND CAN
TOLERATE A SNIP HERE AND THERE.

BUT PRUNING ISN'T JUST ABOUT CREATING A BEAUTIFUL, SHAPELY PLANT.

It's often something that can help them stay healthy, grow more purposefully, and—should something go terribly awry—

bring them back from the brink of death.

WHEN YOU CUT AWAY THE PARTS THAT ARE NO LONGER WORKING FOR YOU, YOU FREE UP ENERGY AND RESOURCES TO SPEND WHERE THEY CAN BE MOST USEFUL.

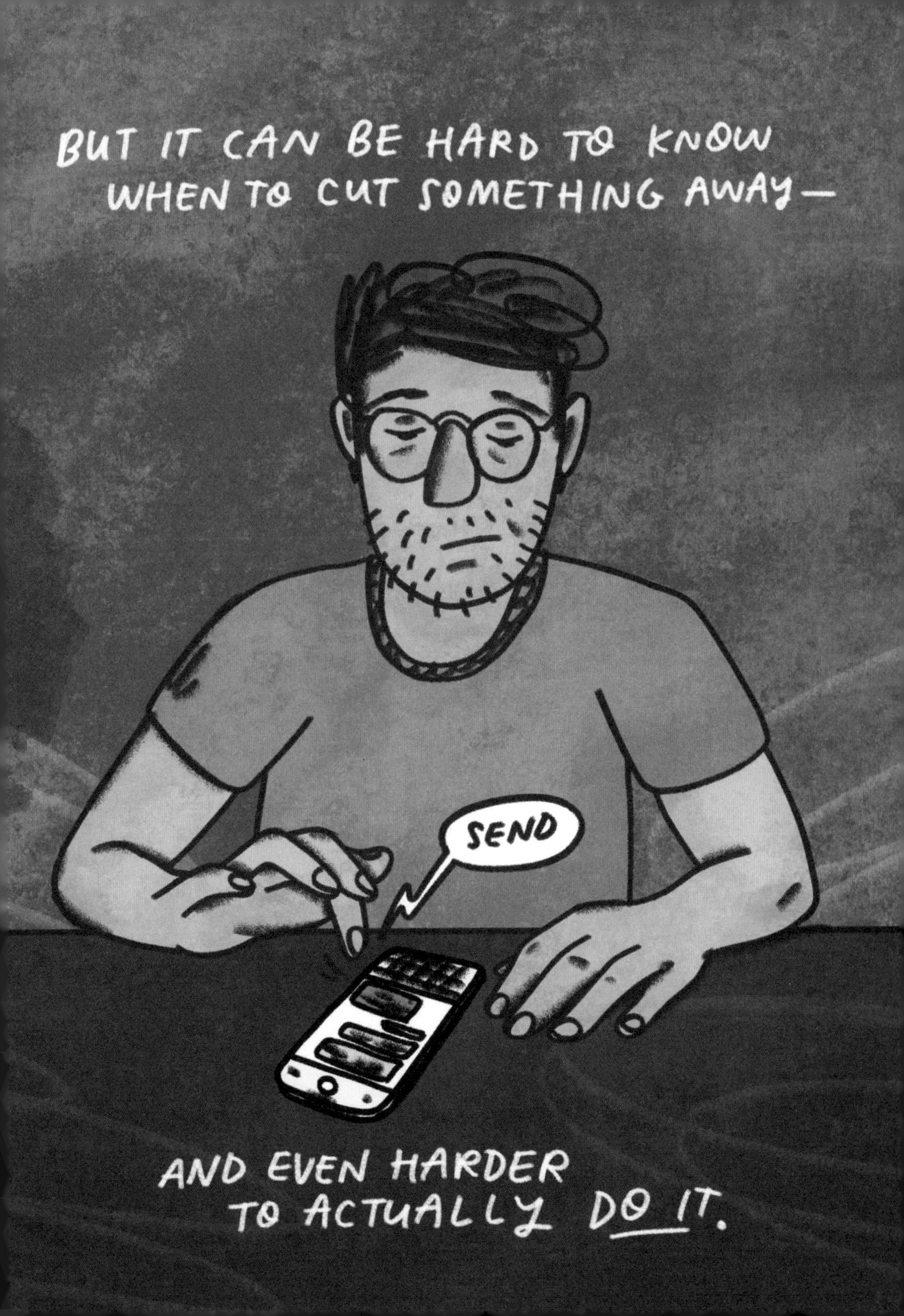
BUT IT CAN BE HARD TO KNOW
WHEN TO CUT SOMETHING AWAY—
SEND
AND EVEN HARDER
TO ACTUALLY DO IT.

REDIRECT YOUR ENERGY

Imagine a young orange tree. Just a few years old, a couple of scrawny branches, immature but well on its way. It might put out dozens of flowers in the spring in an attempt to make dozens of oranges. But it's too grand an undertaking for such a small tree; it simply doesn't have the resources it needs to bring that many fruits to maturity, and so they all wither and drop before they've barely had a chance to grow. And all that energy it spent is gone.

But if most of the tiny oranges are pruned as they begin to form, leaving just a couple intact, the tree will have a much easier time bringing them to maturity. It knows precisely where to focus its limited energy and it isn't spreading itself too thin. It can manage a couple of oranges and still have plenty of energy left to develop its roots, thicken its trunk, and expand its foliage—all things that will help it grow even more fruits in the future.

In this way, thoughtful pruning early on can set a tree up for a long, prolific life.

SOMETIMES A PLANT MAY NEED TO BE CUT BACK ENTIRELY, ALL THE WAY DOWN TO THE ROOTS.

This can feel like a devastating loss; the space the plant once occupied is empty. Its foliage is gone, its life visibly diminished.

IT IS OKAY TO GRIEVE THIS LOSS.

BUT TRY NOT TO DWELL ON IT.

It may well have been necessary for ~~your~~ survival.

ER...THE ^PLANT'S

By cutting it back,
you're providing it a
new opportunity,
a chance for rebirth.
With patience and
time, it will grow back
stronger and livelier
than ever before.

PRUNING MAY SEEM DESTRUCTIVE, BUT IT'S ALWAYS PERFORMED WITH FUTURE GROWTH IN MIND.

You might find that cutting away the bulk of your growth makes room for something stronger and more supportive to grow in its place.

Syringa vulgaris

HOW TO PRUNE— AND GROW BACK STRONGER

STEP 1
ASSESS WHAT'S WEIGHING YOU DOWN

A good pruning requires intention and a little bit of intuition to know what to cut back and when.

More often than not, this requires admitting that something you love isn't working anymore.

THIS IS NEVER EASY.

WHAT IS TROUBLING YOU THAT YOU CAN TRIM AWAY?

What dead weight are you still clinging to?

Whether it's a relationship that's not working, a painting you can't seem to finish, or a fiddle-leaf fig that's lost one too many leaves,

IF YOUR ENERGY WOULD BE BETTER SPENT SOMEWHERE MORE FRUITFUL, YOU DESERVE TO MOVE ON.

LET IT GO

Take a deep breath and shrug it off your shoulders. Set it down gently and say goodbye. It's not coming with you on your next journey.

Mourn what you have let go, but don't forget what remains. It's natural that this weight feels like a part of you, but you are still whole without it.

FOCUS ON THIS FEELING OF LIGHTNESS. CONSIDER THE INFINITE PROMISE THAT THIS EMPTINESS HOLDS.

THINK OF THE COLD, BARREN GROUND IN WINTER AND HOW IT BREAKS OPEN AND BURSTS INTO LIFE EVERY SPRING.

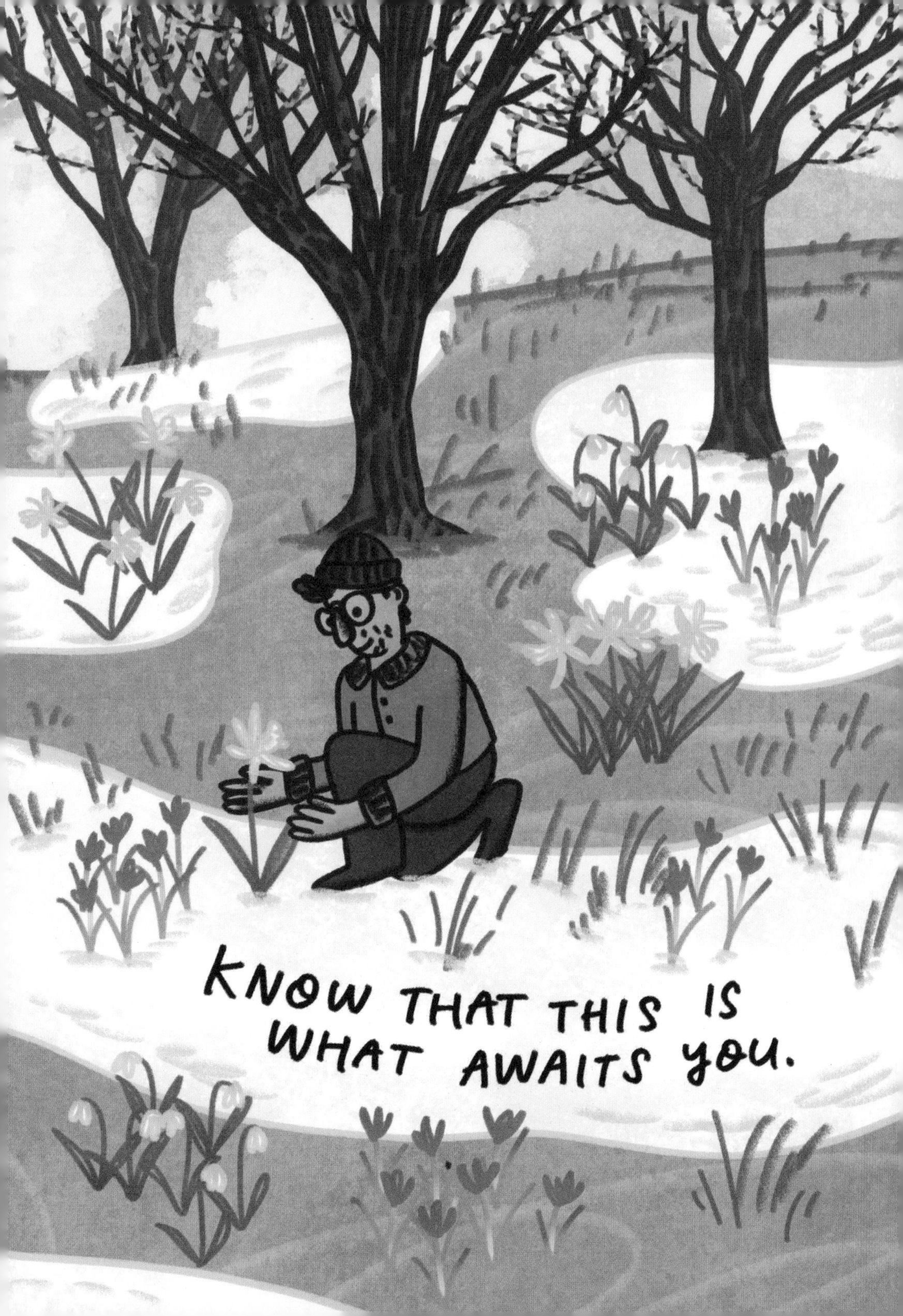
KNOW THAT THIS IS
WHAT AWAITS YOU.

BEGIN AGAIN

THE TRICK TO STARTING OVER IS UNDERSTANDING THAT IT'S A <u>MYTH</u>.

When you've come this far,
you are never starting from nothing:
Everything you've done up to this point—
the seeds you've tended, the soil you've tilled,
the roots you've spread—they are all still contributing.

Pruning yourself down to the roots can
feel like giving everything up.

BUT ALL THOSE THINGS YOU'VE LEARNED ALONG THE WAY WILL SERVE AS A ROAD MAP FOR YOUR FUTURE GROWTH.

Even a dead branch that had to be cut
away is an important reminder for how
you want to grow in the future.

What is cut away is just a piece of a much larger picture. The bright display of green will come back soon, and in the meantime, you are wide and deep and alive, with your roots stretching out beneath you.

YOU ARE STILL WHOLE.

YOU ALWAYS HAVE BEEN.

As this new path unfolds—as you grow
into this wild, new shape—the heart of you
remains, equipped with the knowledge and
understanding of everything that's come before.

IT'S NOT SO
DIFFERENT
THAN STARTING
FROM A SEED.

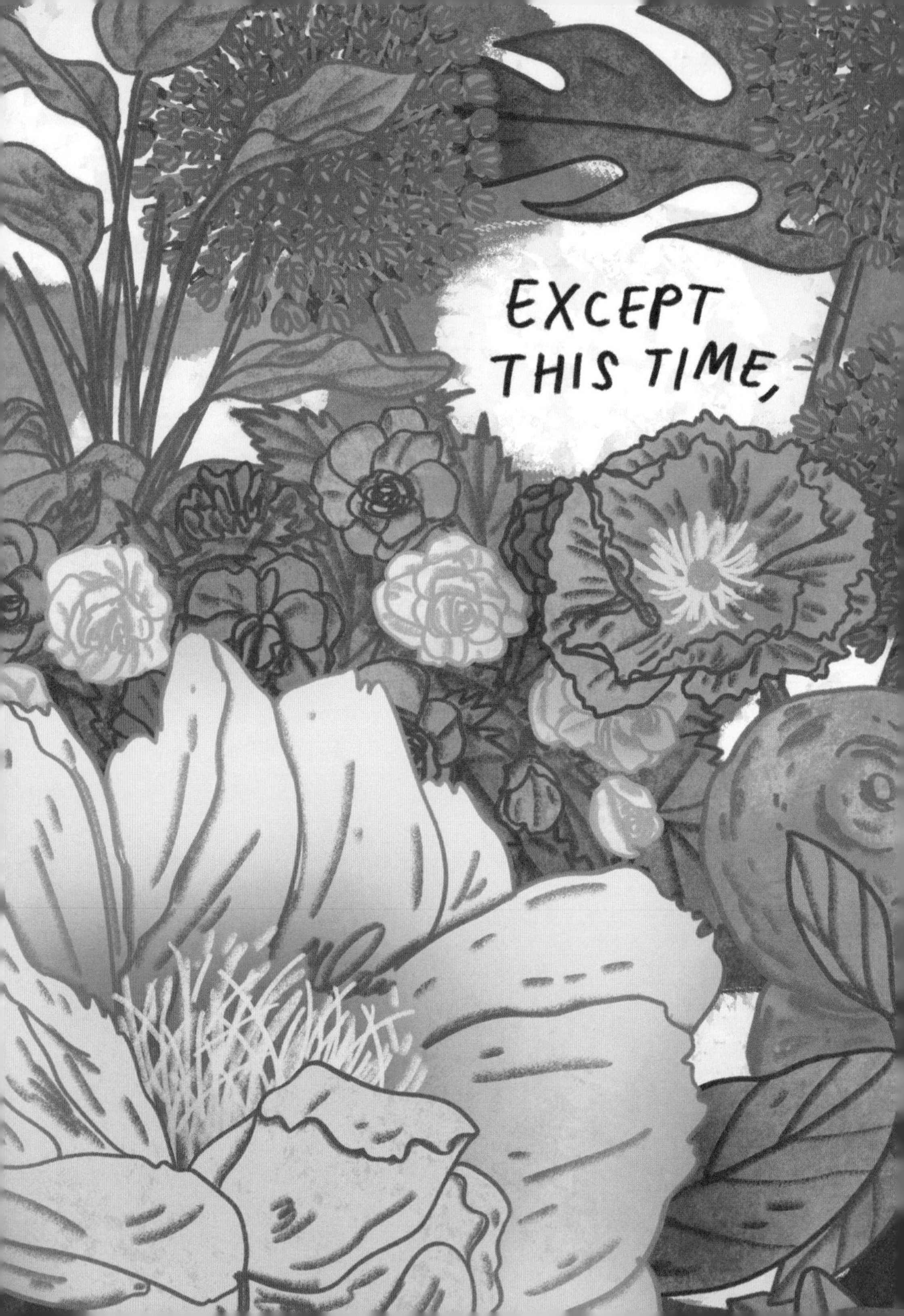
EXCEPT
THIS TIME,

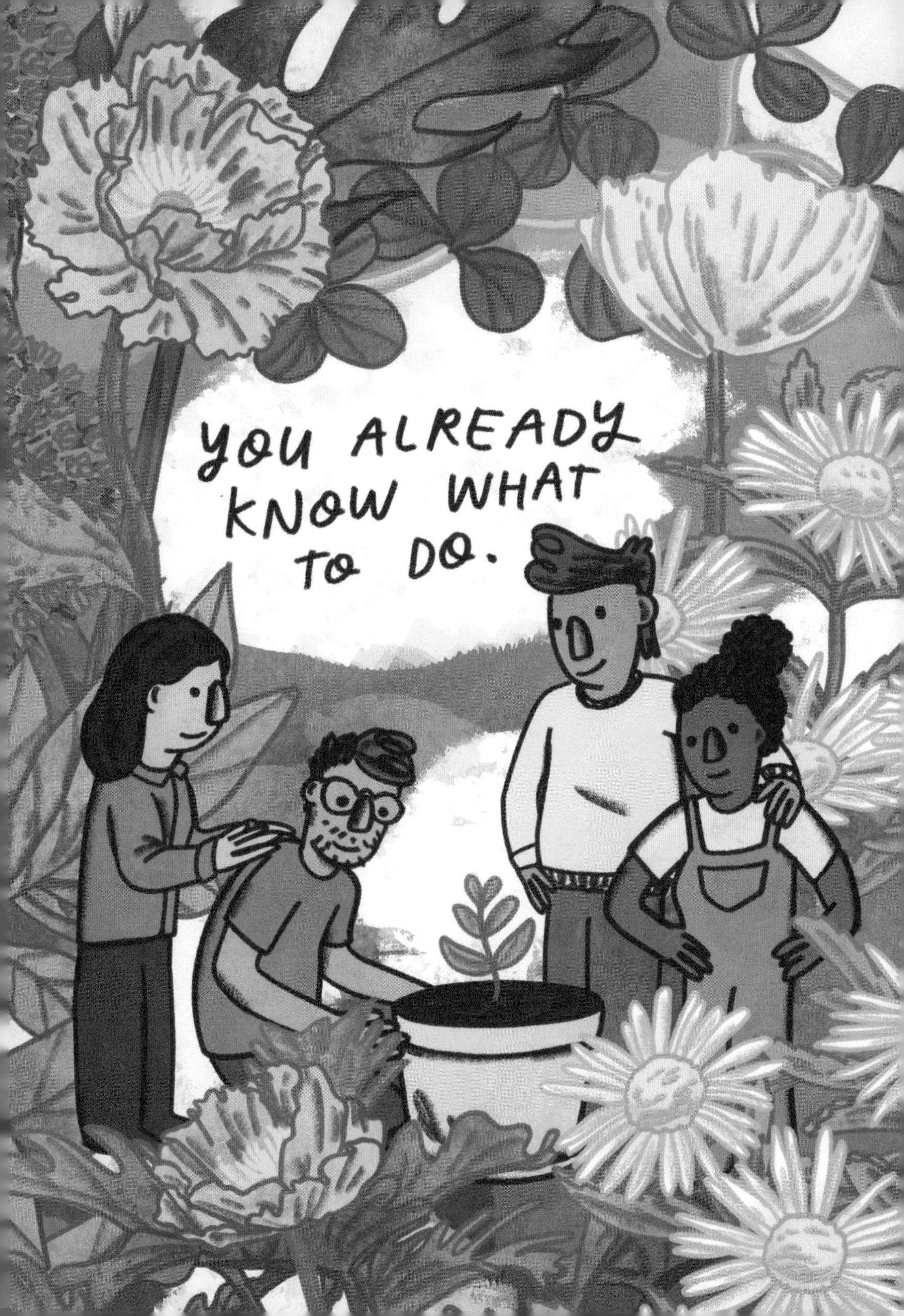
YOU ALREADY KNOW WHAT TO DO.

ACKNOWLEDGMENTS

The idea for this book was a seed like any other, and it could not have come to be in your hands today without a great deal of help.

To Ian Epstein, who, for as long as I have known him, has held each seed of mine, no matter how small, as a precious, worthy thing.

To my family, who have continued to provide me with a rich and nourishing field in which to grow.

To my friends, whose unbending support has been a trellis for my growth long before this seed existed, who helped ease my (frequent) doubts and celebrate my successes: Amanda Kohr, Katy Beyer, Macki Weaver, Gregory Glazier, Tavia Odinak, Sophie Golden, Mary Jane Weedman, and so many more. I love you all.

To Cindy Uh, my extraordinary agent, who immediately saw the strength of this seed and fought for it every step of the way. To Sara Neville, my editor, for believing in this book from the beginning and for giving me the freedom to fulfill my vision of it. And to the whole team at Clarkson Potter for helping it to grow beyond my wildest imaginings: Jessie Kaye, Danielle Deschenes, Abby Oladipo, Luisa Francavilla, and Chloe Aryeh.

To the countless scholars and gardeners and creators who came before me, whose research and art and hours spent digging in the dirt helped show me how much was possible.

FROM MY ROOTS TO MY CROWN, THANK YOU.

Alex Testere is a writer, illustrator, and avid
gardener. He lives with his partner and
an ever-growing menagerie of plants in
upstate New York. This is his first book.

All rights reserved.
Published in the United States by Clarkson Potter/
Publishers, an imprint of Random House, a division
of Penguin Random House LLC, New York.
ClarksonPotter.com
RandomHouseBooks.com

CLARKSON POTTER is a trademark and
POTTER with colophon is a registered
trademark of Penguin Random House LLC.

Library of Congress Cataloging-in-
Publication Data is available.

ISBN 978-0-593-57813-1
Ebook ISBN 978-0-593-57814-8

Printed in China

Editor: Sara Neville
Designer: Alex Testere
Design Manager: Jessie Kaye
Production Editor: Abby Oladipo
Production Manager: Luisa Francavilla
Copy Editor: Natalie Blachere
Marketer: Chloe Aryeh
Publicist: Felix Cruz

10 9 8 7 6 5 4 3 2 1

First Edition

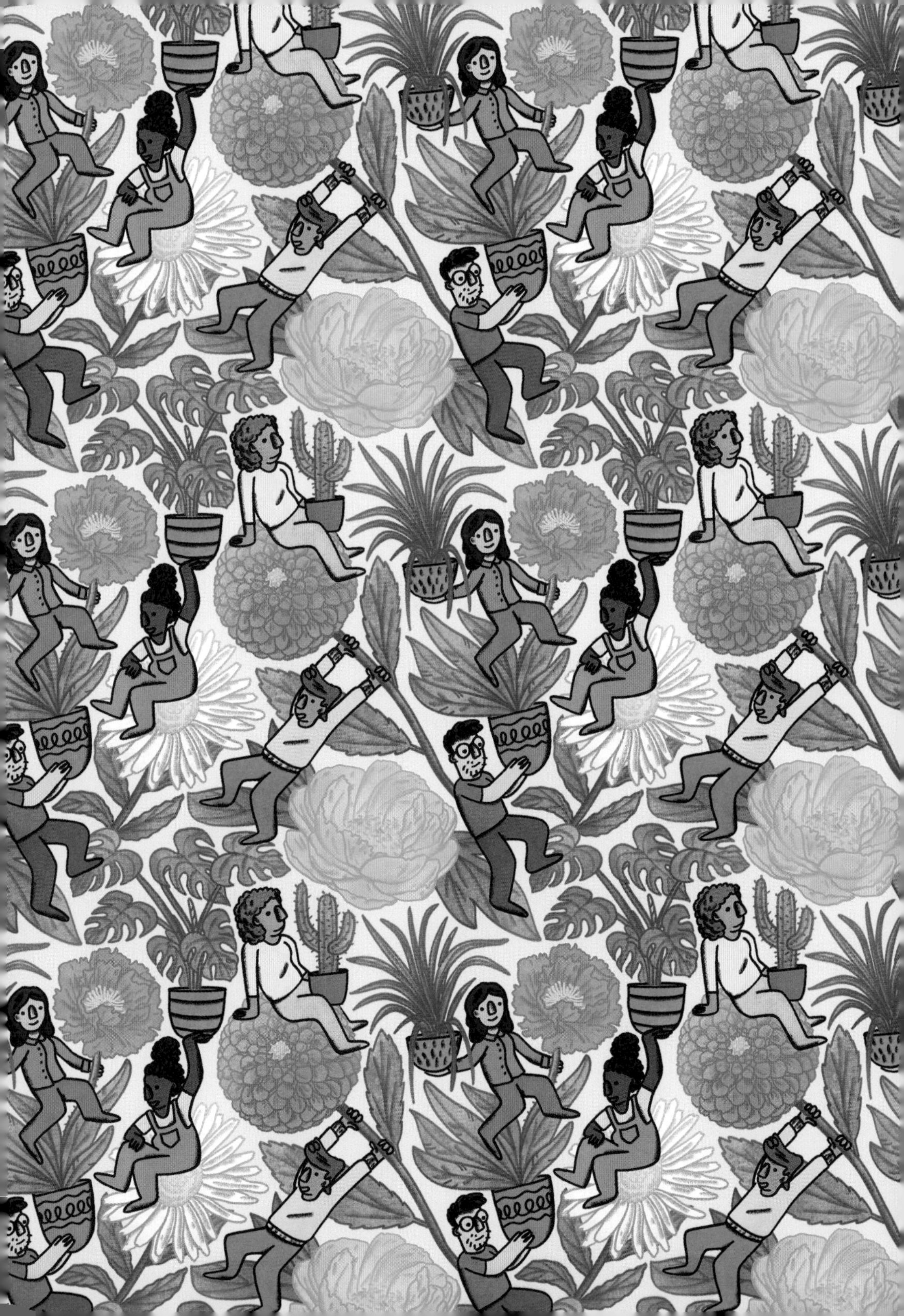

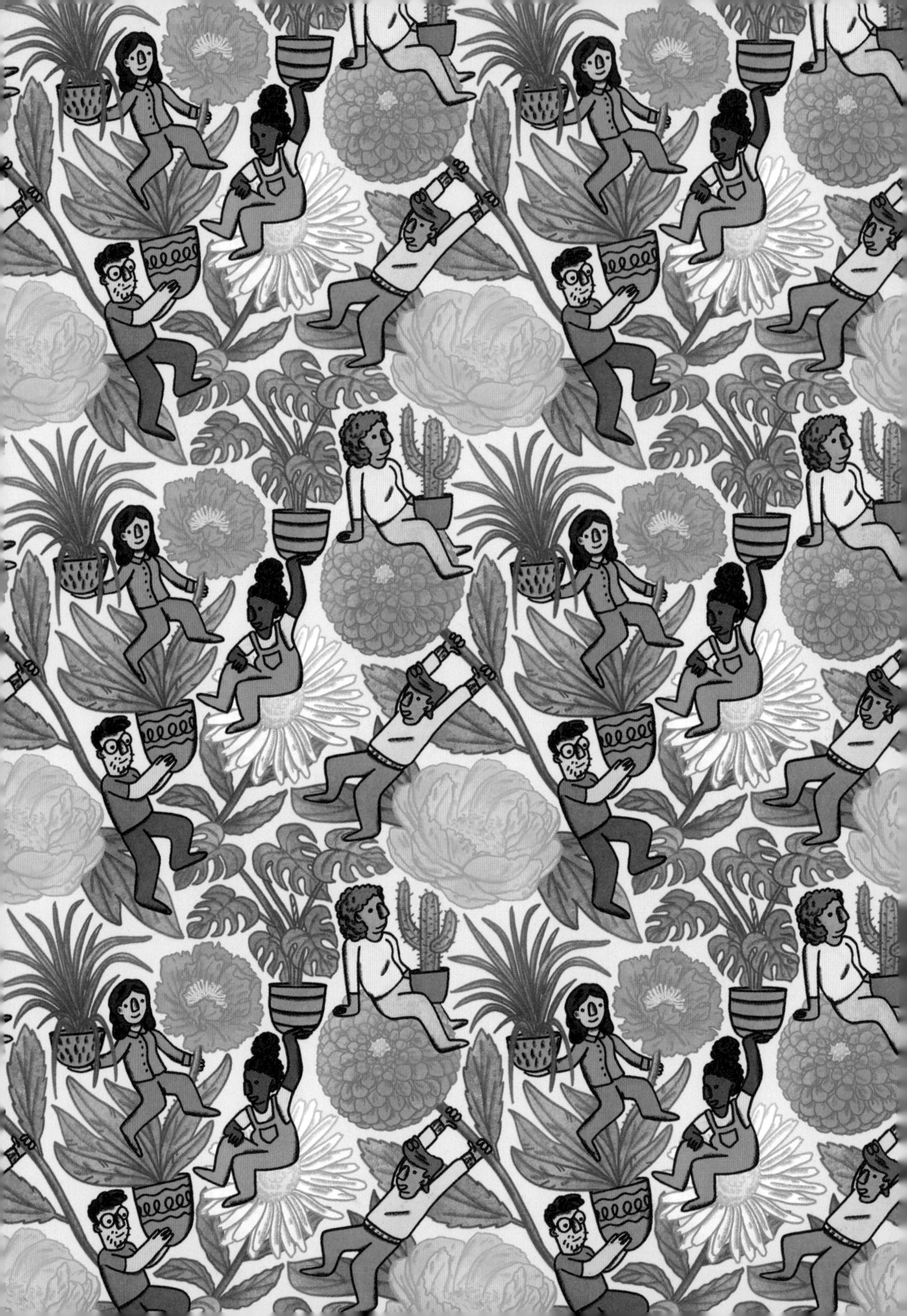